PRESENTED TO:

_____

From:

_____

Date:

_____

CATHOLIC PRAYERS

For All Occasions

EDITED BY JACQUELYN LINDSEY

www.osv.com
Our Sunday Visitor Publishing Division
Our Sunday Visitor, Inc.
Huntington, Indiana 46750

For other credits and sources, see "Acknowledgments," page 349 and "Notes (Sources for Texts)," page 353.

Cover design: Chelsea Alt
Cover art: cross and background © 2016 Thinkstock
Interior design: Sherri L. Hoffman

PRINTED IN THE UNITED STATES OF AMERICA

ABOUT THE AUTHOR

Jacquelyn Lindsey was a longtime editor for Our Sunday Visitor. She continues to edit *LEAVES* magazine for the Mariannhill Missionaries. She served as the editor for a number of prayer books published by Our Sunday Visitor, including:

- **Catholic Family Prayer Book**
- **Prayer Book for Catholics**
- **Catholic Pocket Prayer Book**
- **Catholic Prayer Book,
  Large Print Edition**

She is a devoted wife, mother, and grandmother.

For Don

TABLE OF CONTENTS

BASIC PRAYERS

Amen.

(Means: "So be it.")

The Sign of the Cross
In the name of the Father,
and of the Son,
and of the Holy Spirit.
Amen.

The Lord's Prayer (Our Father)
Our Father, who art in heaven,
hallowed be thy name;
thy kingdom come;
thy will be done
on earth as it is in heaven.
Give us this day our daily bread;
and forgive us our trespasses
as we forgive those
who trespass against us;
and lead us not into temptation,
but deliver us from evil.
Amen.

(See Matthew 6:9-13.)

The Lord's Prayer
(Contemporary version)

Our Father in heaven,
may your name be held holy;
your kingdom come;
your will be done
on earth as in heaven.
Give us this day our daily bread.
Forgive us our sins
as we forgive those who sin against us.
Save us from the time of trial
and deliver us from evil.
Amen.

The Hail Mary

Hail Mary, full of grace.
The Lord is with thee.
Blessed art thou among women,
and blessed is the fruit of thy womb, Jesus.

Holy Mary, Mother of God,
pray for us sinners,
now and at the hour of our death.
Amen.

(See Luke 1:28, 42.)

The Hail Mary
(Contemporary version)

Hail Mary, full of grace.
The Lord is with you.
Blessed are you among women,
and blessed is the fruit of your womb, Jesus.

Holy Mary, Mother of God,
pray for us sinners,
now and at the hour of our death.
Amen.

The Glory Be
(The *Doxology*)

Glory be to the Father,
and to the Son,
and to the Holy Spirit.

As it was in the beginning,
is now, and ever shall be,
world without end.
Amen.

The Glory Be
(Contemporary version)

Glory to the Father,
and to the Son,
and to the Holy Spirit.

As it was in the beginning,
is now and will be forever.
Amen.

Acts of Faith, Hope, and Charity (Love)

Act of Faith

O my God, I firmly believe that you are one God in three divine Persons, Father, Son and Holy Spirit; I believe that your divine Son became man and died for our sins, and that he shall come to judge the living and the dead. I believe these and all the truths that the holy Catholic Church teaches, because you have revealed them, who can neither deceive nor be deceived.

Act of Hope

O my God, relying on your almighty power and infinite mercy and promises, I hope to obtain pardon for my sins, the help of your grace, and life everlasting, through the merits of Jesus Christ, my Lord and Redeemer.

Act of Charity
(Act of Love)

O my God, I love you above all things, with my whole heart and soul, because you are all-good and worthy of all love. I love my neighbor as myself for the love of you. I forgive all who have injured me and ask pardon of all whom I have injured.

(See 1 Corinthians 13:13.)

Act of Contrition

O my God, I am heartily sorry for having offended you, and I detest all my sins, because of your just punishments, but most of all because they offend you, my God, who are all good and deserving of all my love. I firmly resolve, with the help of your grace, to sin no more and to avoid the near occasions of sin. Amen.

The Apostles' Creed

I believe in God,
the Father almighty,
Creator of heaven and earth,
and in Jesus Christ, his only Son, our Lord,
who was conceived by the Holy Spirit,
born of the Virgin Mary,
suffered under Pontius Pilate,
was crucified, died and was buried;
he descended into hell;
on the third day he rose again from the dead;

he ascended into heaven,
and is seated at the right hand
   of God the Father almighty;
from there he will come to judge
   the living and the dead.
I believe in the Holy Spirit,
the holy catholic Church,
the communion of saints,
the forgiveness of sins,
the resurrection of the body,
and life everlasting. Amen.[1]

BLESSED TRINITY

Te Deum

You are God: we praise you;
You are the Lord: we acclaim you;
You are the eternal Father:
All creation worships you.

To you all angels, all the powers of heaven,
Cherubim and Seraphim, sing in endless praise:
   Holy, holy, holy Lord, God of power and
     might,
   heaven and earth are full of your glory.

The glorious company of apostles praise you.
The noble fellowship of prophets praise you.
The white-robed army of martyrs praise you.

Throughout the world the holy Church acclaims
   you:
   Father, of majesty unbounded,
   your true and only Son, worthy of all
     worship,
   and the Holy Spirit, advocate and guide.

You, Christ, are the king of glory,
the eternal Son of the Father.

When you became man to set us free
you did not spurn the Virgin's womb.

You overcame the sting of death,
and opened the kingdom of heaven to all
    believers.

You are seated at God's right hand in glory.
We believe that you will come, and be our
    judge.

Come then, Lord, and help your people,
bought with the price of your own blood,
and bring us with your saints
to glory everlasting.[1]

Holy God, We Praise Thy Name

Holy God, we praise thy name!
Lord of all, we bow before thee;
All on earth thy scepter claim,
All in heav'n above adore thee;
Infinite thy vast domain,
Everlasting is thy reign.

Hark! the loud celestial hymn
Angel choirs above are raising;
Cherubim and Seraphim
In unceasing chorus praising,

Fill the heav'ns with sweet accord:
Holy, holy, holy Lord!

Lo! the apostolic train
Join the sacred Name to hallow;
Prophets swell the loud refrain,
And the white-robed martyrs follow;
And from morn to set of sun,
Through the Church the song goes on.

Holy Father, Holy Son,
Holy Spirit, Three we name thee,
While in essence only One,
Undivided God we claim thee,
And adoring bend the knee,
While we own the mystery.

(This prayer, an adaptation by Father Clarence A. Walworth, 1820-1900, is an English paraphrase of the Te Deum.*)*

The Divine Praises

Blessed be God.
Blessed be his holy name.
Blessed be Jesus Christ, true God and true man.
Blessed be the name of Jesus.
Blessed be his most sacred heart.
Blessed be his most precious blood.
Blessed be Jesus in the most holy sacrament of
    the altar.

Blessed be the Holy Spirit, the Paraclete.
Blessed be the great mother of God, Mary most
    holy.
Blessed be her holy and immaculate conception.
Blessed be her glorious assumption.
Blessed be the name of Mary, virgin and
    mother.
Blessed be St. Joseph, her most chaste spouse.
Blessed be God in his angels and in his saints.

Some add this anonymous prayer:

May the Heart of Jesus, in the most Blessed
    Sacrament,
Be praised, adored, and loved, with grateful
    affection
At every moment in the tabernacles of the
    world.
Even to the end of time.
Amen.

*(Dating back to the eighteenth century, the Divine
Praises are used to honor the Blessed Sacrament.)*

The Little Litany
Heart of my Creator, perfect me.
Heart of my Redeemer, answer for me.
Heart of my Father, govern me.
Heart of my Judge, pardon me.
Heart of my Advocate, plead for me.

Heart of my Master, teach me.
Heart of my Pastor, guard me.
Heart of my faith Friend, rest in me.
Heart wounded for my love, receive me.
Sacred Heart of Jesus dying on the Cross,
　　save me.

PRAYERS TO GOD THE FATHER

Acceptance of God's Will

In all things may the most holy, the most just, and
the most lovable will of God be done, praised, and
exalted above all forever. Your will be done, O
Lord, your will be done. The Lord has given, and
the Lord has taken away; blessed be the name of
the Lord now and always. Amen.[2]

Prayer of St. Louis-Marie Grignon de Montfort

Our Father in heaven, you completely fill heaven
and earth with the immensity of your being; you
are present everywhere; you are in the saints by
your glory, in the damned by your justice, in the
good by your grace, even in sinners by your patience, tolerating them. Grant that we may always
remember that we come from you and that we may
live as your true children. Grant that we may set
our true course according to your will and never

swerve from you. Grant that we may use our every power, our hearts and souls and strength to tend toward you, and you alone.

(St. Louis-Marie Grignion de Montfort, 1673-1716, a French priest who founded the Sisters of Divine Wisdom and Missionaries of the Company of Mary, was particularly devoted to the Blessed Virgin Mary. Feast: April 28.)

A Prayer to God the Father

God be in my head
and in my understanding.
God be in my eyes
and in my looking;
God be in my mouth
and in my speaking.
God be in my heart
and in my thinking.
God be at my end
and my departing.

(From the Sarum Primer, *152.)*

A Prayer of St. Thomas Aquinas

Grant me grace,
O merciful God,
to desire ardently all that is pleasing to you,
to examine it prudently,
to acknowledge it truthfully,

and to accomplish it perfectly,
for the praise and glory of your name.
Amen.[3]

A Prayer from the *Imitation of Christ*

(Book III, 50)

O Lord God, holy Father,
be you now and forever blessed.
For as you will,
    so it has been done;
and what you do is good.
Let your servant rejoice in you,
not in myself or in any other.
You alone are my true joy.
You are my hope and my crown.
You are my gladness and my honor.
O Lord,
what has your servant
    but what has been received from you without
        deserving it?
Yours are the things that you have given and
    have made.
Amen.

(The Imitation of Christ *is a classic work of spiritual
and moral theology attributed to Thomas à Kempis,
c. 1380-1471.)*

Consecration to God
by St. Ignatius Loyola

Take, O Lord, and receive all my liberty, my memory, my understanding, and my whole will. You have given me all that I am and all that I possess; I surrender it all to you that you may dispose of it according to your will. Give me only your love and your grace; with these I will be rich enough and will have no more to desire.

Amen.

Teach Me, My Lord
Attributed to Bl. John Henry Newman

Teach me, my Lord, to be sweet and gentle in all the events of life: in disappointments, in the thoughtlessness of others, in the insincerity of those I trusted, in the unfaithfulness of those on whom I relied.

Let me put myself aside, to think of the happiness of others, to hide my little pains and heartaches, so that I may be the only one to suffer from them.

Teach me to profit by the suffering that comes across my path. Let me so use it that it may mellow me, not harden or embitter me; that it may make me patient, not irritable; that it may make me broad in my forgiveness, not narrow, or haughty and overbearing.

May no one be less good for having come within my influence; no one less pure, less true, less kind, less noble for having been a fellow-traveler in our journey toward eternal life.

As I go from one distraction to another, let me whisper from time to time, a word of love to you. May my life be lived in the supernatural, full of power for good, and strong in its purpose of sanctity.

——— PRAYERS TO JESUS ———

Prayer of St. Augustine

Lord Jesus, let me know myself and know you,
And desire nothing, save only you.
Let me hate myself and love you.
Let me do everything for the sake of you.
Let me humble myself and exalt you.
Let me die to myself and live in you.
Let me accept whatever happens as from you.
Let me banish self and follow you.
Let me fly from myself and take refuge in you,
That I may deserve to be defended by you.
Let me fear for myself, let me fear you,
And let me be among those who are chosen
    by you.
Let me distrust myself and put my trust in you.
Let me be willing to obey for the sake of you.
Let me cling to nothing, save only to you,
And let me be poor because of you.
Call me, that I may see you,
And forever enjoy you. Amen.

Prayer of St. Andrew

O good Cross, made beautiful by the body of the Lord: long have I desired you, ardently have I loved you, unceasingly have I sought you out; and now you are ready for my eager soul. Receive me from among men and restore me to my Master, so that he — who, by means of you, in dying redeemed me — may receive me.

Amen.

(St. Andrew, first century, was one of the Twelve Apostles. Feast: November 30.)

Prayer to the Infant Jesus of Prague

O miraculous Infant Jesus, prostrate before your sacred image, we beseech you to cast a merciful look on our troubled hearts. Let your tender Heart, so inclined to pity, be softened by our prayers, and grant us that grace for which we ardently implore you. Take from us all affliction and despair, all trials and misfortunes with which we are laden. For your sacred infancy's sake, hear our prayers and send us consolation and aid, that we may praise you, with the Father and the Holy Spirit, forever and ever.

Amen.[4]

Prayer to the Sacred Heart of Jesus

By Bl. John Henry Newman

Most sacred, most loving Heart of Jesus, you are concealed in the Holy Eucharist, and you bear for us still. Now, as then, you say: "With desire I have desired." I worship you with all my best love and awe, with fervent affection, with my most subdued, most resolved will. For a while you take up your abode within me. O make my heart beat with your Heart! Purify it of all that is earthly, all that is proud and sensual, of all perversity, of all disorder. So fill it with you, that neither the events of the day, nor the circumstances of the time, may have the power to ruffle it; but that in your love and your fear, it may have peace.

Amen.[5]

Act of Dedication of the Human Race

Most sweet Jesus, Redeemer of the human race, look down upon us humbly prostrate before Your Altar (outside of church or oratory say: in Your presence). We are Yours, and Yours we wish to be; but to be more surely united to You, behold, each one of us this day freely dedicates himself to Your Most Sacred Heart. Many, indeed, have never known Thee; many, too, despising Your precepts have rejected You. Have mercy on them all, most merciful Jesus, and draw them to Your

Sacred Heart. Be King, O Lord, not only of the faithful who have never forsaken You, but also of the prodigal sons who have abandoned You; grant that they may quickly return to their Father's house, lest they perish of wretchedness and hunger. Be Thou King of those whom heresy holds in error or discord keeps aloof; call them back to the harbor of truth and the unity of faith, so that soon there may be but one fold and one Shepherd. Be King of all those who even now sit in the shadow of idolatry, and refuse not to bring them into the light of Your kingdom. Look, finally, with eyes of pity upon the children of that race, which was for so long a time Your chosen people; and let Your Blood, which was once invoked upon them in vengeance, now descend upon them also in a cleansing flood of redemption and eternal life. Grant, O Lord, to Your Church assurance of freedom and immunity from harm; unto all nations give an ordered tranquility; bring it to pass that from pole to pole the earth may resound with one cry: Praise to the divine Heart that wrought our salvation; to It be honor and glory forever and ever.

Amen.

Prayer for Daily Neglects

Eternal Father, I offer you the Sacred Heart of Jesus, with all Its love, all Its sufferings, and all Its merits.

First — to expiate all the sins I have committed this day and during all my life.

Glory be ...

Second — to purify the good I have done badly this day and during all my life.

Glory be ...

Third — to supply for the good I ought to have done, and that I have neglected this day and during all my life.

Glory be ...

Prayer of Thanksgiving

We render thanks unto you, O Christ our God, who of your goodness have bestowed upon us the Food for the sanctification of our lives; keep us through It holy and without blame under your divine protection; feed us in the pastures of your holy and good pleasure, that, being strengthened against all snares of the devil, we may be deemed worthy to hear your holy voice, and follow you, the one victorious and true Shepherd, and to receive from you that place which has been prepared for us in the Kingdom of Heaven. For you, O our God and Lord and Savior Jesus Christ, are blessed with the Father and the Holy Spirit now, and for ever, and world without end. Amen.[6]

— PRAYERS TO THE HOLY SPIRIT—

Prayer to the Holy Spirit

Come, Holy Spirit, fill the hearts of your
    faithful.
And kindle in them the fire of your love.
Send forth your Spirit and they shall be created.
And you will renew the face of the earth.

Lord, by the light of the Holy Spirit
you taught the hearts of your faithful.
In the same Spirit
help us to relish what is right
and always rejoice in your consolation.
We ask this through Christ our Lord.
Amen.

A Prayer for Light

O Holy Spirit of God,
    take me as your disciple.
    Guide me, illuminate me, sanctify me.

Bind my hands that they may do no evil.
Cover my eyes that they may see it no more.
Sanctify my heart that evil may not dwell
    within me.

Be my guide;
    wherever you lead me, I will go;
    whatever you forbid me, I will renounce;
    and whatever you command me in your
      strength, I will do.
    Lead me then to the fullness of your truth.
    Amen.

Veni, Sancte Spiritus

Holy Spirit, Lord of life,
From your clear celestial height
Your pure beaming radiance give.

Come, O Father of the poor;
Come, with treasures that endure;
Come, O light of all who live.

You of all consolers best,
Visiting the troubled breast,
True refreshing peace bestow.

You in toil our comfort sweet,
Pleasant coolness in the heat,
Solace in the midst of woe.

Light immortal, Light divine,
Visit now these hearts of thine
And our inmost being fill.

If you take your grace away,
Nothing pure in us will stay;
All our good is turned to ill.

Heal our wounds, our strength renew;
On our dryness, pour your dew:
Wash the stains of guilt away.

Bend the stubborn heart and will;
Melt the frozen, warm the chill;
Guide the steps that go astray.

You, on those who evermore
Confess you and still adore,
In your sevenfold gift descend.

Give them comfort when they die,
Give them life with you on high;
Give them joys that never end.
Amen.

Prayer of St. Augustine

Breathe in me, Holy Spirit, that all my thoughts
    may be holy.
Act in me, Holy Spirit, that my work too may
    be holy.

Draw my heart, Holy Spirit, that I may love
only what is holy.
Strengthen me, Holy Spirit, to defend all that is
holy.
Guard me, Holy Spirit, that I may always be
holy.

Come, Holy Spirit, Creator Blest
(*Veni, Creator Spiritus*)

Come, Holy Spirit, Creator blest,
and in our souls take up Your rest;
come with Your grace and heavenly aid
to fill the hearts which You have made.

O comforter, to You we cry,
O heavenly gift of God Most High,
O fount of life and fire of love,
and sweet anointing from above.

You in Your sevenfold gifts are known;
You, finger of God's hand we own;
You, promise of the Father, You
Who does the tongue with power imbue.

Kindle our sense from above,
and make our hearts o'erflow with love;
with patience firm and virtue high
the weakness of our flesh supply.

Far from us drive the foe we dread,
and grant us Your peace instead;
so shall we not, with You for guide,
turn from the path of life aside.

Oh, may Your grace on us bestow
the Father and the Son to know;
and You, through endless times confessed,
of both the eternal Spirit blest.

Now to the Father and the Son,
Who rose from death, be glory given,
with You, O Holy Comforter,
henceforth by all in earth and heaven. Amen.

BLESSED VIRGIN MARY

Sub Tuum Praesidium

We fly to your patronage,
  O holy Mother of God;
despise not our petitions in our necessities,
  but deliver us from all danger,
O glorious and blessed Virgin.
Amen.

The *Memorare*

Remember, O most gracious Virgin Mary, that never was it known that anyone who fled to your protection, implored your help, or sought your intercession was left unaided.

Inspired by this confidence I fly unto you, O virgin of virgins, my Mother. To you do I come, before you I stand, sinful and sorrowful. O Mother of the Word Incarnate, despise not my petitions, but in your mercy, hear and answer me.

Amen.

Hail, Holy Queen
(*Salve Regina*)

Hail, holy Queen, Mother of Mercy. Hail, our life, our sweetness and our hope. To you do we cry, poor banished children of Eve. To you do we send up our sighs, mourning, and weeping in this valley of tears. Turn, then, most gracious advocate, your eyes of mercy toward us, and after this, our exile, show unto us the blessed fruit of your womb, Jesus. O clement, O loving, O sweet Virgin Mary.

Queen of Heaven
(*Regina Coeli*)

V. O Queen of Heaven, rejoice, alleluia.
R. For he whom you were privileged to bear, alleluia.
V. Has risen as he said, alleluia.
R. Pray for us to God, alleluia.
V. Rejoice and be glad, O Virgin Mary, alleluia.
R. For the Lord has truly risen, alleluia.

Let us pray: O God, who gave joy to the world through the Resurrection of your Son, our Lord Jesus Christ, grant that we may obtain, through His Virgin Mother, Mary, the joys of everlasting life. Through the same Christ our Lord. Amen.

(During the Easter season, the Regina Coeli *is used instead of the usual Angelus prayer.)*

Hail, Queen of the Heavens
(*Ave Regina Caelorum*)

Hail, Queen of the heavens!
Hail, Empress of the angels!
Hail, Root of Jesse, gate of morn!
From you the world's true Light was born.

Rejoice, glorious Virgin
Lovelier than all the other virgins in heaven.
You are fairer than all the fair,
Plead with Christ, our sins to spare.
Amen.

Loving Mother of the Redeemer
(*Alma Redemptoris Mater*)

O loving Mother of the Redeemer,
Gate of Heaven, Star of the Sea,
Assist your people who have fallen,
    yet strive to rise again.
To the wonder of nature, you bore your Creator,
Yet remained a Virgin, after as before,
You who received Gabriel's joyful greeting,
    have pity on us poor sinners.
Amen.

(This is an evening prayer often used during the Advent and Christmas seasons.)

The *Stabat Mater*

At the Cross her station keeping
Stood the mournful Mother weeping,
   Close to Jesus to the last.

Through her heart his sorrow sharing,
All his bitter anguish bearing,
   Lo! the piercing sword had passed.

For his people's sins rejected,
Saw her Jesus unprotected,
   Saw with thorns, with scourges rent.

Saw her Son from judgment taken,
Her beloved in death forsaken,
   Till his spirit forth he sent.

Jesus, may your Cross defend me,
And your Mother's prayer befriend me.
   Let me die in your embrace.

When to dust my dust returns
Grant a soul, which for you yearns,
   In your Paradise a place.
Amen.

Prayer to Our Lady, Help of Christians

By St. John Bosco

O heavenly Lady, help of Christians, I come to
you, for you never refuse help to anyone. Mary,

help of Christians, you have often answered the prayers of nations. You have helped the Pope, bishops, priests, religious, all Christians. Whenever those who love you put their hope in you, you hurry to them with a mother's love. Your greatest wish is to help the holy Church of your Son still here on earth.

My mother, my hope, O Lady, help of Christians, make me live in the love of your holy Son, Jesus Christ. Help me in my every need.[1]

Miraculous Medal Prayer

O Mary conceived without sin,
pray for us who have recourse to you.

(This prayer was given to St. Catherine Labouré, 1806-1876, during an apparition of the Blessed Mother, in Paris, in 1830. St. Catherine's feast day is November 28.)

Pope St. John Paul II's Prayer to Mary

O Mary,
bright dawn of the new world,
Mother of the living,
to you do we entrust the *cause of life*:

Look down, O Mother,
upon the vast numbers
of babies not allowed to be born,
of the poor whose lives are made difficult,

of men and women who are
victims of brutal violence,
of the elderly and the sick killed
by indifference or out of misguided mercy.

Grant that all who believe in your Son
may proclaim the Gospel of life
with honesty and love
to the people of our time.

Obtain for them the grace
to accept that Gospel
as a gift ever new,
the joy of *celebrating it* with gratitude
throughout their lives
and the courage to *bear witness to it*
resolutely, in order to build,
together with all people of good will,
the civilization of truth and love,
to the praise and glory of God,
the Creator and lover of life.[2]

(Pope St. John Paul II's feast day is October 22.)

The Rosary

The Rosary can be prayed year round, but special
effort should be made during October, the month
of the Rosary.

- On the crucifix, pray: The Apostles' Creed
- On the first large bead, pray: One Our Father

Praying the Rosary

Second Mystery:
Our Father, etc.

Glory Be to
the Father

Hail Mary
(ten times)

First Mystery:
Our Father

Glory Be to
the Father

Conclusion:
Hail, Holy Queen

Hail Mary
(three times)

Our Father

Apostles' Creed

- On the next three small beads, pray: Three Hail Marys
- Pray: One Glory Be

Each decade of the Rosary consists of one Our Father (on the large beads), ten Hail Marys (on the small beads), and one Glory Be. Many then add the Fátima invocation: "O my Jesus, forgive us our sins, save us from the fires of hell, and lead all souls to heaven, especially those most in need of thy mercy."

The Joyful Mysteries
(Said on Mondays and Saturdays)
1. The Annunciation of the Lord to Mary (Lk 1:26-38)
2. The Visitation of Our Lady with St. Elizabeth (Lk 1:39-56)
3. The Nativity of Our Lord (Mt 1:18-25; Lk 2:1-20)
4. The Presentation of the Christ Child in the Temple (Lk 2:22-39)
5. The Finding of the Child Jesus in the Temple (Lk 2:41-52)

The Luminous Mysteries
(Said on Thursdays)
1. The Baptism of the Lord (Mt 3:13-17).
2. The Wedding Feast at Cana (Jn 2:1-11)
3. The Preaching of the Kingdom of God (Mk 1:14-15)

4. The Transfiguration of the Lord (Lk 9:33-36)
5. The Institution of the Eucharist (Mt 26:26-28)

The Sorrowful Mysteries

(Said on Tuesdays and Fridays)

1. The Agony in the Garden (Mk 14:32-42)
2. The Scourging of Jesus (Jn 19:1)
3. The Crowning with Thorns (Mk 15:16-20)
4. The Carrying of the Cross (Jn 19:12-17)
5. The Crucifixion (Mt 27:33-56; Mk 15:22-41; Lk 23:33-49; Jn 19:18-30)

The Glorious Mysteries

(Said on Wednesdays and Sundays)

1. The Resurrection (Mt 28:1-10; Mk 16:1-8; Lk 24:1-12; Jn 20)
2. The Ascension (Lk 24:50-53; Acts 1:1-12)
3. The Descent of the Holy Spirit at Pentecost (Acts 2:1-4)
4. The Assumption of the Blessed Virgin Mary (Song 2:8-14)
5. The Coronation of the Blessed Virgin Mary (Rev 12:1-4)

CONCLUDING PRAYER: Hail, holy Queen, Mother of Mercy. Hail, our life, our sweetness and our hope. To you do we cry, poor banished children of Eve. To you do we send up our sighs, mourning, and weeping in this valley of tears. Turn, then, most gracious advocate, your eyes of mercy toward us, and after this, our exile, show unto us the blessed fruit of your womb, Jesus. O clement, O loving, O sweet Virgin Mary.

V. Pray for us, O Holy Mother of God.
R. That we made be made worthy of the promises of Christ.

Let us pray: O God, whose only begotten Son, by his life, death, and resurrection has purchased for us the rewards of eternal life, grant, we beseech you, that we, who meditate on these mysteries of the most holy Rosary of the Blessed Virgin Mary, may both imitate what they contain and obtain what they promise, by the same Christ Our Lord.
   Amen.

The Seven Sorrows of Mary
   I. The Prophecy of Simeon (Lk 2:22-35)
   II. The Flight into Egypt (Mt 2:1-15)
   III. The Loss of the Child Jesus in the Temple (Lk 2:41-52)
   IV. Mary Meets Jesus on the Way to Calvary (Lk 23:27-31)
   V. Jesus Dies on the Cross (Mt 27:45-50; Mk 15:37; Lk 23:46; Jn 19:30)
   VI. Mary Receives the Body of Jesus in Her Arms
   VII. The Body of Jesus Is Placed in the Tomb (Mt 27:59-60; Mk 15:46; Lk 23:53; Jn 19:38-42)

SAINTS AND HOLY ONES

(PRAYERS TO — AND BY — THEM)

St. Aloysius Gonzaga

O Holy Mary, my Lady, into your blessed trust and safe keeping and into the depths of your mercy, I commend my soul and body this day, every day of my life, and at the hour of my death. To you I entrust all my hopes and consolations, all my trials and miseries, my life and the end of my life. By your most holy intercession and by your merits, may all my actions be directed and disposed according to your will and the Will of your divine Son. Amen.

(St. Aloysius Gonzaga, 1568-1591, was an Italian Jesuit who died young. Patron of Catholic youth. Feast: June 21.)

St. Alphonsus Liguori

Prayer for Five Graces

Eternal Father, your Son has promised that you would grant all the graces we ask of you in His name. Trusting in this promise, and in the name and through the merits of Jesus Christ, I ask of you five graces: First, I ask pardon for all offenses I have committed, for which I am sorry with all my heart, because I have offended your infinite goodness. Second, I ask for your divine Light, which will enable me to see the vanity of all the things of this earth, and see also your infinite greatness and goodness. Third, I ask for a share in your love, so that I can detach myself from all creatures, especially from myself, and love only your holy will. Fourth, grant me the grace to have confidence in the merits of Jesus Christ and in the intercession of Mary. Fifth, I ask for the grace of perseverance, knowing that whenever I call on you for assistance, you will answer my call and come to my aid; I fear only that I will neglect to turn to you in time of need, and thus bring myself to ruin. Grant me the grace to pray always, O Eternal Father, in the name of Jesus. Amen.[1]

(This prayer is attributed to St. Alphonsus Liguori, 1696-1787. He was an Italian bishop and founder of the Redemptorists, and he is a Doctor of the Church. Patron of confessors and moralists. Feast: August 1.)

St. Anne

Good St. Anne, obtain for me an increase of faith in the great mystery of the Holy Eucharist. Help me to see in this great Sacrament Christ our High Priest, making real for me the saving grace of His death on the cross; feeding my soul with His Flesh and Blood so that I may live in Him and He in me; producing the unity of the people of God and gathering His Church together. By your powerful intercession with God, help me to center my life around the altar that I may inherit the promise of the Lord: "He who eats my flesh and drinks my blood has life everlasting." Amen.

(St. Anne is the mother of the Virgin Mary, Mother of God. Feast: July 26.)

St. Anselm of Canterbury

I Am Desperate

I am desperate for your love, Lord. My heart is aflame with fervent passion. When I remember the good things you have done, my heart burns with desire to embrace you. I thirst for you; I hunger for you; I long for you; I sigh for you. I am jealous of your love. What shall I say to you? What can I do for you? Where shall I seek you? I am sick for your love. The joy of my heart turns to dust. My happy laughter is reduced to ashes. I want you. I hope for you. My soul is like a widow, bereft of you. Turn to me, and see my tears. Come now, Lord, and I will be comforted. Show me your face, and I shall be saved. Enter my room, and I shall be satisfied. Reveal your beauty, and my joy will be complete.

Searching for God

O Lord, my God, teach my heart this day where and how to see you, where and how to find you. You have made me and remade me, and you have bestowed on me all the good things I possess, and still I do not know you. I have not yet done that for which I was made. Teach me to seek you, for I cannot seek you unless you teach me, or find you unless you show yourself to me. Let me seek you in my desire; let me desire you in my seeking. Let me find you by loving you; let me love you when I find you.[2]

(This prayer is attributed to St. Anselm, 1033-1109, Italian Benedictine, archbishop of Canterbury, and Doctor of the Church. He is called the Father of Scholasticism. Feast: April 21.)

St. Anthony of Padua

Prayer to Recover Lost Things

O blessed St. Anthony, the grace of God has made you a powerful advocate in all our needs and the patron for the restoring of things lost or stolen. I turn to you today with childlike love and deep confidence. You are the counselor of the erring, the comforter of the troubled, the healer of the sick, the refuge of the fallen. You have helped countless children of God to find the things they have lost — material things and, more importantly, the things of the spirit: faith and hope and love. I come to you with confidence. Help me in my present need. I recommend what I have lost to your care, in the hope that God will restore it to me if it is His holy will. Amen.

(St. Anthony of Padua, 1195-1231, a Franciscan who is called the "Wonder Worker," was proclaimed a Doctor of the Church. Patron for finding lost items. Feast: June 13.)

St. Augustine

For behold, you were within me, and I outside; and I sought you outside and in my ugliness fell upon those lovely things that you have made. You were with me, and I was not with you. I was kept from you by those things, yet had they not been in you, they would not have been at all. You called and cried to me and broke upon my deafness; and you sent forth your light and shone upon me, and chased away my blindness; you breathed fragrance upon me, and I drew in my breath and did not pant for you; you touched me, and I have burned for your peace.[3]

(St. Augustine, 354-430, was the bishop of Hippo in North Africa. His writings in philosophy and theology made lasting contributions to the Church. Feast: August 28.)

St. Basil the Great

O Lord our God, we beseech you, to ask for the gift we need. Steer the ship of our life to yourself, the quiet harbor of all storm-stressed souls. Show us the course which we are to take. Renew in us the spirit of docility. Let your Spirit curb our fickleness; guide and strengthen us to perform what is for our own good, to keep your commandments and ever to rejoice in your glorious and vivifying presence. Yours is the glory and praise for all eternity. Amen.

The Ship of Life

Steer the ship of my life, Lord, to your quiet harbor, where I can be safe from the storms of sin and conflict. Show me the course I should take. Renew in me the gift of discernment, so that I can see the right direction in which I should go. And give me the strength and the courage to choose the right course, even when the sea is rough and the waves are high, knowing that through enduring hardship and danger in your name we shall find comfort and peace. Amen.

(St. Basil the Great, c. 330-379, was the bishop of Caesarea. He is a Father and Doctor of the Church and is called the Father of Monasticism in the East. Feast: January 2.)

St. Benedict of Nursia

For Seekers of Faith

Gracious and holy Father, give us the wisdom to discover you, the intelligence to understand you, the diligence to seek after you, the patience to wait for you, eyes to behold you, a heart to meditate on you, and a life to proclaim you, through the power of the spirit of Jesus, our Lord.

(This prayer was inspired by St. Benedict.)

Instruments of Good Works
(From St. Benedict's Rule)

O Lord,
I place myself in your hands
and dedicate myself to you.

I pledge myself to do your will in all things —
To love the Lord God with all my heart, all my
    soul, all my strength.
Not to kill,
Not to steal,
Not to covet,
Not to bear false witness,
To honor all persons.
Not to do to another what I should not wish
    done to myself.
To chastise the body.
Not to seek after pleasures.

To love fasting.
To relieve the poor.
To clothe the naked.
To visit the sick.

To bury the dead.
To help in trouble.
To console the sorrowing.
To hold myself aloof from worldly ways.
To prefer nothing to the love of Christ.

Not to give way to anger.
Not to foster a desire for revenge.
Not to entertain deceit in the heart.
Not to make a false peace.
Not to forsake charity.
Not to swear, lest I swear falsely.

To speak the truth with heart and tongue.
Not to return evil for evil.
To do no injury, indeed, even to bear patiently
    any injury done to me,
to love my enemies.
Not to curse those who curse me, but rather to
    bless them.
To bear persecution for justice' sake.

Not to be proud.
Not to be given to intoxicating drink.
Not to be an overeater.

Not to be lazy.
Not to be slothful.
Not to be a murmurer.
Not to be a detractor.

To put my trust in God.
To refer the good I see in myself to God.
To refer any evil I see in myself to myself.
To fear the day of judgment.
To be in dread of hell.
To desire eternal life with spiritual longing.
To keep death before my eyes daily.
To keep constant watch over my actions.

To remember that God sees me everywhere.
To call upon Christ for defense against evil
    thoughts that arise in my heart.
To guard my tongue against wicked speech.
To avoid much speaking.
To avoid idle talk.

Not to seek to appear clever.
To read only what is good to read.
To pray often.
To ask forgiveness daily for my sins, and to seek
    ways to amend my life.
To obey my superiors in all things rightful.
Not to desire to be thought holy, but to seek
    holiness.

To fulfill the commandments of God by good
   works.
To love chastity.
To hate no one.
Not to be jealous or envious of anyone.
Not to love strife.
Not to love pride.
To honor the aged.
To pray for my enemies.
To make peace after a quarrel, before the setting
   of the sun.

Never to despair of your mercy, O God of
   Mercy.
Amen.

*(St. Benedict of Nursia, c. 480-547, founder of the
Benedictine Order, is known as the great Father of
Western Monasticism. Patron of Europe. Feast: July
11.)*

St. Benedict Joseph Labre

Jesus Christ, King of Glory, came in peace. God
was made man. The Word was made flesh. Christ
was born of the Virgin Mary. Christ walked in
peace through the midst of them. Christ was crucified. Christ died. Christ was buried. Christ rose
again. Christ ascended into heaven. Christ conquers. Christ reigns. Christ commands. May Christ
defend us from all evil. Jesus is with us. Amen.

(St. Benedict Joseph Labre, 1748-1783, the "beggar of Rome," was known for his dedication to the Forty Hours Devotion. Feast: April 16.)

St. Bernadette Soubirous

O St. Bernadette, who, as a meek and pure child, did eighteen times at Lourdes contemplate the beauty of the Immaculate Mother of God and received her messages, and who afterwards wished to hide yourself from the world in the convent of Nevers, and to offer thyself there as a victim for the conversion of sinners, obtain for us the grace of purity, simplicity, and mortification that we also may attain to the vision of God and of Mary in Heaven. Amen.

(St. Bernadette, 1844-1879, received visions of the Blessed Virgin Mary — who called herself the Immaculate Conception — at Lourdes, France, where many miracles have since been reported. Feast: February 18.)

St. Bernard of Clairvaux

Oh, how good and pleasant a thing it is
    to dwell in the Heart of Jesus!
Who is there that does not love
    a heart so wounded?
Who can refuse a return of love
    to a heart so loving!
Amen.

The Sweetness of Divine Love

Jesus, how sweet is the very thought of you! You fill my heart with joy. The sweetness of your love surpasses the sweetness of honey. Nothing sweeter than you can be described; no words can express the joy of your love. Only those who have tasted your love for themselves can comprehend it. In your love you listen to all my prayers, even when my wishes are childish, my words confused, and my thoughts foolish. And you answer my prayers, not according to my own misdirected desires, which would bring only bitter misery; but according to my real needs, which brings me sweet joy. Thank you, Jesus, for giving yourself to me. Amen.

(St. Bernard of Clairvaux, 1090-1153, French monastic reformer, is called the Mellifluous Doctor. Feast: August 20.)

St. Bernardine of Siena

Jesus, Name full of glory, grace, love, and strength! You are the refuge of those who repent, our banner of warfare in this life, the medicine of souls, the comfort of those who mourn, the delight of those who believe, the light of those who preach the true faith, the wages of those who toil, the healing of the sick.

To You our devotion aspires; by You our prayers are received; we delight in contemplating

You. O Name of Jesus, You are the glory of all the
saints for eternity. Amen.

*(St. Bernardine of Siena, 1380-1444, an Italian
Franciscan, had a special devotion to the Holy Name
of Jesus. Feast: May 20.)*

St. Bonaventure

O holy Lord,
Father almighty,
everlasting God,
for your sake and for that of your Son, who
    suffered and died for me:
through the merits of the Virgin Mary and all
    the saints,
grant that I may love you above all else,
acknowledging my unworthiness,
and complaining of nothing but my faults.
Amen.

Prayer to St. Anthony of Padua

Let those who seek for miracles invoke the glorious
St. Anthony. At his word all evils disappear: death
and error, demons and leprosy; the sick rise up
restored to perfect health.

His word and presence calm the troubled
seas and break the captive's chain, lost things are
found, and old and young never appeal to him in
vain. Perils are averted, hostilities cease.

If proof be needed of the truth of this, listen to

the testimony of the people of Padua, eyewitnesses
to these wondrous deeds.

St. Anthony of Padua, pray for us.

*(This second prayer is attributed to St. Bonaventure,
1221-1274 — contemplative, mystic, Italian Franciscan — also known as the Seraphic Doctor. Feast:
July 15.)*

St. Brigid of Ireland

I would like the angels of heaven to be
    among us.
I would like the abundance of peace.
I would like full vessels of charity.
I would like rich treasures of mercy.
I would like cheerfulness to preside over all.
I would like the friends of heaven to be gathered
    around us from all parts.
I would like myself to be a rent-payer to the
    Lord; that I should suffer distress and that
    He would bestow a good blessing upon me.

*(St. Brigid, c. 453-523, was baptized by St. Patrick
and went on to found convents throughout Ireland.
Feast: February 1.)*

St. Catherine of Siena

O tender Father,
you gave me more, much more
than I ever thought to ask for.

I realize that our human desires
can never really match
what you long to give us.

Thanks,
and again thanks, O Father,
for having granted my petitions, and
that which I never realized I needed
or petitioned.
Amen.

(St. Catherine of Siena, 1347-1380, an Italian member of the Third Order of St. Dominic, is a Doctor of the Church. Feast: April 29.)

St. Cecilia

Dear St. Cecilia, one thing we know for certain about you is that you became a heroic martyr in fidelity to your divine Bridegroom.

We do not know that you were a musician, but we are told that you heard angels sing.

Inspire musicians to gladden the hearts of people by filling the air with God's gift of music and reminding them of the divine Musician who created all beauty.

(St. Cecilia, second-third centuries, was a Roman virgin and martyr. Patron of music. Feast: November 22.)

St. Christopher

Dear Saint, you have inherited a beautiful name
— Christ bearer — as a result of a wonderful
legend that while carrying people across a raging
stream you also carried the Child Jesus. Teach us
to be true Christ bearers to those who do not know
Him. Protect all drivers who often transport those
who bear Christ within them.

Amen.

*(St. Christopher, died c. 251 — whose name, in
Greek, means "Christ-bearer" — is one of the Four-
teen Holy Helpers. Patron of travelers, archers, and
protection against storms. Feast: July 25.)*

St. Clare

O Blessed St. Clare, your life shines like a beacon
and casts its light down the ages of the Church to
guide the way of Christ. Look with compassion on
the poor and humble who call on you for help. As
you bow before your Eucharistic Lord in Heaven,
speak to Him of my afflicted body and my broken
spirit. Ask Him to heal me and to wash away my
sins in His precious Blood.

Great Servant of Christ, remember the needs
of my family and all those I pray for. Defend us
from everything that would threaten our Holy
Catholic faith. Hear the cry of the poor and make
it a song of intercession, rising from your poor

heart to the Eucharistic Heart of Jesus, our Healer, our Savior, and our Lord.

Amen.

(St. Clare of Assisi, 1194-1253, founded the Poor Clares. Patron of eye-disease sufferers, television, goldsmiths, and laundry. Feast: August 11.)

St. Clement of Rome

Prayer for Divine Assistance

We beg you, Lord, to help and to defend us. Deliver the oppressed, pity the insignificant, raise the fallen, show yourself to the needy, heal the sick, bring back those of your people who have gone astray, feed the hungry, lift up the weak, take off the prisoners' chains. May every nation come to know that you alone are God, that Jesus Christ is your Child, that we are your people, the sheep that you pasture.[4]

(This prayer was inspired by St. Clement of Rome, pope 92-99, a martyr invoked against disasters at sea, storms, and lightning. Feast: November 23.)

St. Clement of Alexandria

To the Divine Tutor

Be kind to your little children, Lord. Be a gentle teacher, patient with our weakness and stupidity. And give us the strength and discernment to do what you tell us, and so grow in your likeness. May we all live in the peace that comes from you. May we journey towards your city, sailing through the waters of sin untouched by the waves, borne serenely along by the Holy Spirit. Night and day may we give you praise and thanks, because you have shown us that all things belong to you, and all blessings are gifts from you. To you, the essence of wisdom, the foundation of truth, be glory forevermore.

(This prayer was inspired by St. Clement of Alexandria, c. 150-215 — confessor, teacher, and author. Feast: December 4.)

St. Cyprian of Carthage

For All Needs

We pray to you, Lord, with honest hearts, in tune with one another, entreating you with sighs and tears, as befits our humble position — placed, as we are, between the spiritually weak who have no concern for you and the saints who stand firm and upright before you. We pray that you may soon come to us, leading us from darkness to light, oppression to freedom, misery to joy, conflict to peace. May you drive away the storms and tempests of our lives, and bring gentle calm. We pray that you will care for us, as a father cares for his children. Amen.

(This prayer was inspired by St. Cyprian of Carthage, c. 200-258. Born in Africa, he was the bishop of Carthage and an author. Feast: September 16.)

St. Damien de Veuster

Damien, brother on the journey, happy and generous missionary, who loved the Gospel more than your own life, who for love of Jesus left your family, your homeland, your security, and your dreams.

Teach us to give our lives with joy like yours, to be in solidarity with the outcasts of our world, to celebrate and contemplate the Eucharist as the source of our own commitment.

Help us to love to the very end and, in the strength of the Spirit, to persevere in compassion for the poor and forgotten so that we might be good disciples of Jesus and Mary. Amen.

(St. Damien, 1840-1889, ministered to the lepers of Molokai, Hawaii, eventually contracting the disease and dying of it himself. Pope Benedict XVI declared him a saint October 11, 2009. Feast: May 10.)

St. Edmund

Into your hands, O Lord,
and into the hands of your holy angels,
I commit and entrust this day my soul,
   my relations, my benefactors,
   my friends and my enemies,
    and all your people.

Keep us, O Lord, through this day
by the merits and intercession
   of the Blessed Virgin Mary
   and all the saints,
from all vicious and unruly desires,
from all sins and temptations of the devil,
and from sudden and improvided death
and the pains of hell.
Illuminate my heart
   with the grace of your Holy Spirit;
grant that I may ever be obedient
   to your commandments;
suffer me not to be separated from you,
O Lord Jesus Christ,
who lives and reigns
   with God the Father
   and the same Holy Spirit
forever and ever. Amen.

(This prayer was inspired by St. Edmund of Abingdon, c. 1170-1240, archbishop of Canterbury, England. Feast: November 20.)

St. Frances Xavier Cabrini

Fortify me with the grace of your Holy Spirit and give your peace to my soul that I may be free from all needless anxiety, solicitude, and worry. Help me to desire always that which is pleasing and acceptable to you so that your will may be my will. Amen.

(Note: A longer version of this prayer is on page 241.)

(St. Frances Xavier Cabrini, 1850-1917, an Italian nun who came to the United States and founded the Missionary Sisters of the Sacred Heart. She became a citizen and was the first American citizen to be canonized. Feast: November 13.)

St. Francis de Sales

Your Cross

The everlasting God has in His wisdom foreseen from eternity the cross that He now presents to you as a gift from His inmost Heart. This cross He now sends you He has considered with His all-knowing eyes, understood with His Divine mind, tested with His wise justice, warmed with loving arms and weighed with His own hands to see that it be not one inch too large and not one ounce too heavy for you. He has blessed it with His holy Name, anointed it with His grace, perfumed it with His consolation, taken one last glance at you and your courage, and then sent it to you from heaven, a special greeting from God to you, a gift of the all-merciful love of God. Amen.

(St. Francis de Sales, 1567-1622, bishop of Geneva and devotional writer, is a Doctor of the Church. Patron of Catholic writers and the Catholic press. Feast: January 24.)

St. Francis of Assisi

I believe that you are present in the Blessed Sacrament, O Jesus. I love you and desire you. Come into my heart.

I embrace you; O never leave me. I beg you, O Lord Jesus, that the burning and most sweet power of your love absorb my mind, that I may die through love of your love, since you graciously died for love of my love.

Amen.

(St. Francis, 1181/82-1226, founded the Franciscan Order and received the sacred stigmata. Patron of Italy, Catholic Action, and ecologists. Feast: October 4. This prayer may be used for Spiritual Communion.)

St. Gianna Beretta Molla

Jesus, I promise You to submit myself to all that You permit to befall me, make me only know Your will. My most sweet Jesus, infinitely merciful God, most tender Father of souls, and in a particular way of the most weak, most miserable, most infirm which You carry with special tenderness between Your divine arms, I come to You to ask You, through the love and merits of Your Sacred Heart, the grace to comprehend and to do always Your holy will, the grace to confide in You, the grace to rest securely through time and eternity in Your loving divine arms. Amen.

(St. Gianna Beretta Molla, 1922-1962, an Italian physician, died after forgoing treatment — for the sake of her unborn child — that would have cured her. Patron of mothers and physicians. Feast: April 28.)

St. Gregory Nazianzen

Lord Jesus, you want us to become a living force for all mankind, lights shining in the world. You want us to become radiant lights as we stand beside you, the great light, bathed in your glory, O Light of Heaven.

Let us enjoy more and more the pure and dazzling light of the Holy Trinity, as now we have received, though not in its fullness, a ray of its splendor, proceeding from the one true God, in Christ Jesus our Lord, to whom be glory and power forever and ever. Amen.

(St. Gregory Nazianzen, c. 330-c. 390, archbishop of Constantinople, was known as "the Theologian" and for his fight against heresy. Feast: January 2.)

St. Hildegard of Bingen

Father, Source of Life,
you have bestowed on St. Hildegard of Bingen
many excellent graces.
Help us to follow her example
of meditating on your ineffable Majesty
and to follow you

so that we, amidst the darkness of this world,
recognize the Light of your clarity
to cling to you without fail.
Through our Lord Jesus Christ, your Son,
who lives and reigns with you
in the unity of the Holy Spirit,
one God, forever and ever.
Amen.[5]

(St. Hildegard, 1098-1179, a German mystic, was named Doctor of the Church in 2012 by Pope Benedict XVI. Feast: September 17.)

St. Ignatius Loyola

For a Generous Spirit

Dearest Lord,
teach me to be generous.
Teach me to serve you as you deserve;
to give, and not to count the cost;
to fight, and not to heed the wounds;
to labor, and not to seek to rest;
to give of myself
and not to ask for reward,
except the reward of knowing
that I am doing your will.
Amen.

(St. Ignatius Loyola, 1491-1556, was the founder of the Jesuits, a leader of the Catholic Reformation, and the author of the Spiritual Exercises. *Feast: July 31.)*

St. Isaac Jogues

Jesus, our Brother, you won the heart of St. Isaac Jogues and helped him grow as a caring, courageous person. He dedicated his life to sharing his love for you by carrying the Good News about your love for all people to others.

Remembering the spirit of St. Isaac Jogues, may we all grow in caring and courage. Help each of us, Jesus, to be strong and gentle messengers of your love. Amen.

(St. Isaac Jogues, 1607-1646, and companions — known as the North American Martyrs, Jesuit missionaries from France — were canonized in 1930. Feast: October 19.)

St. John (Don) Bosco

O glorious St. John Bosco, who in order to lead young people to the feet of the divine Master and to mold them in the light of faith and Christian morality did heroically sacrifice yourself to the very end of your life and did set up a proper religious Institute destined to endure and to bring to the farthest boundaries of the earth your glorious work, obtain also for us from Our Lord a holy love for young people who are exposed to so many seductions in order that we may generously spend ourselves in supporting them against the snares of the devil, in keeping them safe from the dangers

of the world, and in guiding them, pure and holy,
in the path that leads to God.

Amen.

*(St. John Bosco, 1815-1888, an Italian priest,
founded the Salesians for the education of boys and
cofounded the Daughters of Mary Help of Christians
for the education of girls. Feast: January 31.)*

Bl. John Henry Newman

Lead, Kindly Light, amid the encircling gloom,
    Lead Thou me on!
The night is dark, and I am far from home —
    Lead Thou me on!
Keep Thou my feet; I do not ask to see
The distant scene — one step enough for me.

I was not ever thus, nor pray'd that Thou
    Shoudst lead me on.
I loved to choose and see my path, but now
    Lead Thou me on!
I loved the garish day, and, in spite of fears,
Pride ruled my will: remember not past years.

So long Thy power hath blest me, sure it still
    Will lead me on,
O'er moor and fen, o'er crag and torrent, till
    The night is gone;
And with the morn those angel faces smile
Which I have loved long since, and lost awhile.

For a Holy Death

May He support us all the day long,
till the shades lengthen and the evening comes,
and the busy world is hushed,
and the fever of life is over,
and our work is done.
Then in His mercy may He give us a safe
    lodging,
and a holy rest and peace at the last.

*(Bl. John Henry Newman, 1801-1890, converted
from the Anglican Church of England and became
a cardinal. He contributed to the rebirth of the
Catholic Church in England. He was beatified on
September 19, 2010. Feast: October 9.)*

St. John of the Cross

Prayer for Peace

O blessed Jesus, give me stillness of soul in You.
Let your mighty calmness reign in me. Rule me,
O You, King of Gentleness, King of Peace.[6]

*(St. John of the Cross, 1542-1591, Spanish, co-
founder of the Discalced Carmelites, is called the
Doctor of Mystical Theology. Feast: December 14.)*

St. John Vianney

I love you, O my God, and my only desire is to love you until the last breath of my life. I love you, O my infinitely lovable God, and I would rather die loving you, than live without loving you. I love you, Lord, and the only grace I ask is to love you eternally. My God, if my tongue cannot say it in every moment that I love you, I want my heart to repeat it to you as often as I draw breath.

How Good It Is to Love You

My Jesus, from all eternity you were pleased to give yourself to us in love. And you planted within us a deep spiritual desire that can only be satisfied by yourself. I may go from here to the other end of the world, from one country to another, from riches to greater riches, from pleasure to pleasure, and still I shall not be content. All the world cannot satisfy the immortal soul. It would be like trying to feed a starving man with a single grain of wheat. We can only be satisfied by setting our hearts, imperfect as they are, on you. We are made to love you; you created us as your lovers. It sometimes happens that the more we know a neighbor, the less we love him. But with you it is quite the opposite. The more we know you, the more we love you. Knowledge of you kindles such a fire in our souls that we have no energy left for worldly desires. My Jesus, how good it is to love you. Let me be like your disciples on Mount Tabor, seeing nothing else but you. Let us be like two bosom friends, neither of whom can ever bear to offend the other.[7]

(St. John Vianney, 1786-1859, French, was dedicated to his priestly vocation. Patron of priests. Feast: August 4.)

St. Joseph

Ave Joseph

Hail, Joseph, filled with divine grace, in whose arms the Savior was carried and under whose eyes He grew up, blessed art thou among men and blessed is Jesus, the Son of thy dear Spouse.

Holy Joseph, chosen to be a father to the Son of God, pray for us in the midst of our cares of family, health, and work, and deign to assist us at the hour of our death.

Amen.

(St. Joseph, d. first century, foster father of Jesus and spouse of Mary, is the patron of the Universal Church, protector of workers, patron of social justice and a happy death. Feasts: March 19 and St. Joseph the Worker on May 1.)

St. Josephine Bakhita

St. Josephine Bakhita, you were sold into slavery
    as a child
and endured untold hardship and suffering.
Once liberated from your physical enslavement,
you found true redemption in your encounter
    with Christ and his Church.

O St. Bakhita, assist all those who are trapped
    in a state of slavery;
Intercede with God on their behalf
so that they will be released from their chains
of captivity.
Those whom man enslaves, let God set free.

Provide comfort to survivors of slavery
and let them look to you as an example of hope
    and faith.
Help all survivors find healing from their
    wounds.
We ask for your prayers and intercessions for
    those enslaved among us. Amen.[8]

*(St. Josephine, c. 1869-1947, was born in Sudan,
sold into slavery as a child, and became free in Italy,
where she entered the Catholic Church and became
a nun. Pope St. John Paul II canonized her October
1, 2000. Feast: February 8.)*

Bl. Julian of Norwich

God, of your goodness, give me yourself, for you are sufficient for me. I cannot properly ask for anything less, to be worthy of you. If I were to ask less, I should always be in want. In you alone do I have all. Amen.

(Bl. Julian, also called Bl. Juliana, c. 1342-c. 1416, was an English mystic. Feast: May 13 [by tradition].)

St. Margaret Mary Alacoque

Prayer to the Sacred Heart of Jesus

O Heart of Love,
I put all my trust in you.
For I fear all things
   from my own weakness,
but I hope for all things
   from your goodness.
Amen.

(St. Margaret Mary Alacoque, 1647-1690, French religious, was instrumental in spreading devotion to the Sacred Heart and First Friday devotions. Feast: October 16.)

St. Marguerite Bourgeoys

Marguerite Bourgeoys, you who contributed so greatly to the human and Christian promotion of the family in the New World, continue to protect our homes.

Inspire young couples to prepare in a Christian manner for marriage.

Help husbands and wives to grow in love and in fidelity to their commitments.

Assist parents in the education of their children. Obtain for them the necessary material and spiritual means to provide for their needs.

Come to the help of those whose happiness is threatened or shattered.

Bring joy to unhappy children.

Stimulate and enlighten the zeal of those who, in their respective commitments, devote themselves as you did to the human and Christian promotion of families.

Grant that we may re-discover in the Holy Family an ever living model of family life based on Gospel values, and obtain for us the protection of Jesus, Mary, and Joseph.

Amen.

(St. Marguerite Bourgeoys, 1620-1700, was a French nun who journeyed to Montreal and established the Sisters of the Congrégation de Notre-Dame. Feast: January 12.)

St. Maximilian Maria Kolbe

St. Maximilian, amidst the hate and lonely misery of Auschwitz, you brought love into the lives of fellow captives and sowed the seeds of hope amidst despair. You bore witness to the world by word and deed that "Love alone creates." Help me to become more like you. With the Church and Mary and you, may I proclaim that "Love alone creates." To the hungry and oppressed, the naked and homeless, the scorned and hated, the lonely and despairing, may I proclaim the power of Christ's love, which endures forever and ever. Amen.

(St. Maximilian Maria Kolbe, 1894-1941, a Polish Conventual Franciscan, was a prisoner at Auschwitz who offered his life in exchange for another prisoner. Feast: August 14.)

St. Padre Pio of Pietrelcina

O Lord,
    we ask for a boundless confidence
    and trust in Your divine mercy,
    and the courage to accept
    the crosses and sufferings
    which bring immense goodness
    to our souls and that of Your Church.

Help us to love You
    with a pure and contrite heart,
    and to humble ourselves beneath Your cross,

as we climb the mountain of holiness,
carrying our cross that leads to heavenly glory.

May we receive You
with great faith and love in Holy
Communion,
and allow You to act in us as You desire
for your greater glory.

O Jesus, most adorable Heart
and eternal fountain of Divine Love,
may our prayer find favor before
the Divine Majesty of Your heavenly Father.

(St. Padre Pio of Pietrelcina, 1887-1968, was an Italian Capuchin priest who bore the wounds of the stigmata [the wounds of Christ] for 50 years. He possessed many spiritual gifts. Feast: September 23.)

St. Patrick

Dear St. Patrick, in your humility you called yourself a sinner, but you became a most successful missionary and prompted countless pagans to follow the Savior.

Many of their descendants in turn spread the Good News in numerous foreign lands.

Through your powerful intercession with God, obtain the missionaries we need to continue the work you began.

Amen.

(St. Patrick, 389-461, is known for his missionary work and the conversion of Ireland. Feast: March 17.)

St. Richard of Chichester

Thanks be to you, my Lord Jesus Christ, for all the benefits and blessings which you have given to me, for all the pains and insults which you have borne for me. O most merciful Friend, Brother and Redeemer, may I know you more clearly, love you more dearly, and follow you more nearly, day by day.[9]

(This prayer is attributed to St. Richard of Chichester, 1198-1253, who was an English bishop. Feast: April 3.)

St. Rose Philippine Duchesne

Gracious God, you filled the heart of Philippine Duchesne with charity and missionary zeal, and gave her the desire to make you known to all peoples. Fill us who honor her memory today with that same love and zeal, and extend your kingdom to the ends of the earth. We ask this through Christ our Lord.

Amen.[10]

(St. Rose Philippine Duchesne, 1769-1852, French nun and American missionary, founded the Society of the Sacred Heart. Feast: November 18.)

St. Teresa of Jesus (Ávila)

Lord, grant that I may always allow myself to be guided by you, always follow your plans, and perfectly accomplish your holy will.

Grant that in all things, great and small, today and all the days of my life, I may do whatever you may require of me.

Help me to respond to the slightest prompting of your grace, so that I may be your trustworthy instrument of your honor.

May your will be done in time and eternity — by me, in me, and through me.

Amen.

Let Nothing Disturb You

Let nothing disturb you. Let nothing frighten you. All things pass. God does not change. Patience achieves everything. Whoever has God lacks nothing. God alone suffices.

God has no body now on earth but yours; no hands but yours; no feet but yours. Yours are the eyes through which the compassion of Christ must look out on the world. Yours are the feet with which He is to go about doing good. Yours are the hands with which He is to bless His people.

Amen.

(St. Teresa of Ávila, 1515-1582, Spanish Carmelite nun and first woman Doctor of the Church, reformed the Carmelite Order. Feast: October 15.)

St. Teresa of Calcutta

Dear Jesus, help us to spread your fragrance
    everywhere we go.
Flood our souls with your spirit and life.
Penetrate and possess our whole being so
    utterly
that our lives may only be a radiance of yours.
Shine through us,
and be so in us,
that every soul we come in contact with
may feel your presence in our soul.
Let them look up and see no longer us
but only Jesus!
Stay with us,
and then we shall begin to shine as you
    shine;
so to shine as to be a light to others;
the light, O Jesus, will be all from you,
none of it will be ours;
it will be you, shining on others through us.
Let us thus praise you in the way you love
    best,
by shining on those around us.
Let us preach you without preaching,
not by words but by our example,
by the catching force,
the sympathetic influence of what we do,
the evident fullness of the love our hearts bear
    to you. Amen.[11]

(The preceding prayer, Mother Teresa's favorite, has been attributed to Bl. John Henry Newman.)

Prayer for Daily Service

Make us worthy, Lord, to serve our fellow men throughout the world who live and die in poverty and hunger. Give them through our hands this day their daily bread, and by our understanding love, give peace and joy.[12]

Lord, Open Our Eyes

Lord, open our eyes, that we may see you in our brothers and sisters. Lord, open our ears, that we may hear the cries of the hungry, the cold, the frightened, the oppressed. Lord, open our hearts, that we may love each other as you love us. Renew in us your spirit. Lord, free us and make us one.[13]

Lord, Shake Away My Indifference

Lord, shake away my indifference and insensitivity to the plight of the poor. When I meet you hungry, thirsty or as a stranger, show me how I can give you food or quench your thirst or receive you in my home and in my heart. Show me how I can serve you in the least of your brothers.[14]

(St. Teresa of Calcutta, 1910-1997, founder of the Missionaries of Charity, was canonized a saint on September 4, 2016. Feast: September 5.)

St. Thérèse of Lisieux

Daily Offering to God

My God, I offer you all that I do today
for the intentions and the glory of the Sacred
    Heart of Jesus.
I want to sanctify every beat of my heart,
my thoughts and my simplest works
by uniting them to his infinite merits.
I want to repair for my faults
by casting them into the furnace of his merciful
    love.

O my God!
I ask you for myself and for those dear to me
the grace to fulfill perfectly your holy will
and to accept for love of you
the joys and sorrows of this passing life,
so that one day we may be reunited in Heaven
    for all eternity.
Amen.

*(St. Thérèse of Lisieux, 1873-1897, also called St.
Thérèse of the Child Jesus or "The Little Flower,"
was a French Carmelite nun and is a Doctor of the
Church. Feast: October 1.)*

St. Thomas Aquinas

For All Good Things

Loving God, who sees in us nothing that you have not given yourself, make my body healthy and agile, my mind sharp and clear, my heart joyful and contented, my soul faithful and loving. And surround me with the company of men and angels who share my devotion to you. Above all, let me live in your presence, for with you all fear is banished, and there is only harmony and peace. Let every day combine the beauty of spring, the brightness of summer, the abundance of autumn, and the repose of winter. And at the end of my life on earth, grant that I may come to see and to know you in the fullness of your glory. Amen.

(St. Thomas Aquinas, 1225-1274, was one of the Church's greatest theologians. Devoted to the Blessed Sacrament, he is called the "Angelic Doctor." Feast: January 28.)

Thomas à Kempis

God, our Father, we are exceedingly frail and indisposed to every virtuous and gallant undertaking. Strengthen our weakness, we beseech you, that we may do valiantly in this spiritual war; help us against our own negligence and cowardice, and defend us from the treachery of our unfaithful hearts, for Jesus Christ's sake. Amen.

(Thomas à Kempis, 1380-1471, German monk, is commonly credited to have written the Imitation of Christ.*)*

St. Thomas More

Good Lord, give me the grace, in all my fear and agony, to have recourse to that great fear and wonderful agony that you, my sweet Savior, had at the Mount of Olivet before your most bitter passion, and in the meditation thereof, to conceive ghostly comfort and consolation profitable for my soul.

Almighty God, take from me all vainglorious minds, all appetites of mine own praise, all envy, all covetise, gluttony, sloth and lechery, all wrathful affections, all appetite of revenging, all desire or delight of other folks' harm, all pleasure in provoking any person to wrath and anger, all delight of exprobation or insultation against any persons in their affliction and calamity.

And give me, good Lord, a humble, lowly, quiet, peaceable, patient, charitable, kind, tender and pitiful mind, with all my works, and all my words, and all my thoughts, to have a taste of your Holy, Blessed Spirit.

Give me, good Lord, a full faith, a firm hope, and a fervent charity, a love to the good Lord incomparable above the love to myself; and that I love nothing to your displeasure, but everything in an order to you.

Take from me, good Lord, this lukewarm fashion, or rather key-cold manner of meditation, and this dullness in praying to you. And give me warmth, delight, and quickness in thinking of you.

And give me your grace to long for your holy sacraments, and especially to rejoice in the presence of your very blessed Body, sweet Savior Christ, in the holy sacrament of the altar, and duly to thank you for your gracious visitation therewith, and at that high memorial, with tender compassion, to remember and consider your most bitter passion. Amen.

(St. Thomas More, 1478-1535, was an English chancellor who suffered martyrdom. Feast: June 22.)

St. Vincent Ferrer

Lord Jesus Christ, who wills that no one should perish and to whom supplication is never made without the hope of mercy — for you said with your own holy and blessed lips: All things whatsoever you ask in my name will be done to you — I ask you, O Lord, for the sake of your holy name, to grant me at the hour of death full consciousness and the power of speech, sincere contrition for my sins, true faith, firm hope and perfect charity, that I may be able to say to you with a clean heart: Into your hands, O Lord, I commend my spirit.

You have redeemed me, O God of truth, you who are blessed forever. Amen.[15]

(St. Vincent Ferrer, 1350-1419, was a Spanish Do-minican priest noted for being an excellent preacher. Feast: April 5.)

ANGELS

Angels are mentioned throughout the Bible. Guardian angels are sent by God to guide and protect each one of us. Other angels, such as the archangels, serve as messengers of God to His people on earth. There are traditionally nine orders, or choirs, of angels: Seraphim, Cherubim, Thrones, Dominions, Virtues, Powers, Principalities, Archangels, and Angels.

St. Michael the Archangel

St. Michael, the Archangel, defend us in battle; be our defense against the wickedness and snares of the devil. May God rebuke him, we humbly pray; and do thou, O Prince of the heavenly host, by the power of God, thrust into hell Satan and the other evil spirits who prowl about the world seeking the ruin of souls.

Amen.

(Note: In 1884, Pope Leo XIII wrote the above prayer, which used to be said at the end of every Mass. Pope St. John Paul II asked that Catholics revive the prayer: "I invite you all not to forget it. Pray it so as to be helped in the battle against the forces of darkness and against the spirit of this world.")

(Michael means "Who is like God?"; he is one of the most beloved angels. The prophet Daniel describes him as the prince who stands guard over God's people. He is invoked for his healing and is the patron of police officers. Feast: September 29.)

St. Raphael the Archangel

O God,
send the Archangel Raphael to our assistance.
May he who stands forever praising you
at your throne
present our humble petitions
to be blessed by you.
Through Christ our Lord.
Amen.

(Raphael means "God's Healer"; one of the three angels mentioned by name in Scripture, his story is found in the Book of Tobit. Feast: September 29.)

St. Gabriel the Archangel

O God,
who from among all your angels
chose the Archangel Gabriel
to announce the mystery of the Incarnation,
mercifully grant that we
who solemnly remember him on earth

may feel the benefits of his
patronage in heaven,
who lives and reigns forever and ever.
Amen.

*(Gabriel means "Strength of God"; he appeared to
Zechariah to tell him that his wife Elizabeth would
bear a son; six months later he appeared to the Virgin
Mary to announce that she, too, would give birth to a
son, Jesus; see Luke, chapter 1. Feast: September 29.)*

Prayer to All the Angels

All you holy angels and archangels,
thrones and dominations,
principalities and powers,
the virtues of heaven,
cherubim and seraphim,
praise the Lord forever.
Amen.

Prayers to One's Guardian Angel

Angel of God,
whom God has appointed to be my protector
     against all things evil:
be always at my side, and keep me aware of your
     presence as God's messenger to me all the
     days of my life, for my good.
Pray for me this day and every day of my life in
     this world.
Amen.

Angel sent by God to guide me,
be my light and walk beside me;
be my guardian and protect me;
on the paths of life direct me.

LITANIES

A litany is a form of prayer using repetition of phrases and is sometimes chanted. Most are based on Scripture and developed over time. The Litany of the Saints is sometimes used in the Mass (for baptism and ordination).

Litany of the Holy Name

Lord, have mercy on us.

Lord, have mercy on us.

Christ, have mercy on us.

Christ, have mercy on us.

Jesus, hear us.   **Jesus, graciously hear us.**

God the Father of heaven,   **Have mercy on us.**
God the Son, Redeemer of the world, ...
God the Holy Spirit, ...
Holy Trinity, one God, ...
Jesus, Son of the living God, ...
Jesus, Splendor of the Father, ...
Jesus, Brightness of eternal light, ...
Jesus, King of glory, ...
Jesus, Sun of justice, ...
Jesus, Son of the Virgin Mary, ...

Jesus, most amiable, …   **Have mercy on us.**
Jesus, most admirable, …
Jesus, the mighty God, …
Jesus, Father of the world to come, …
Jesus, Angel of the Great Council, …
Jesus, most powerful, …
Jesus, most patient, …
Jesus, most obedient, …
Jesus, meek and humble of heart, …
Jesus, Lover of chastity, …
Jesus, Lover of us, …
Jesus, God of peace, …
Jesus, Author of life, …
Jesus, Example of virtues, …
Jesus, zealous Lover of souls, …
Jesus, our God, …
Jesus, our Refuge, …
Jesus, Father of the poor, …
Jesus, Treasure of the faithful, …
Jesus, Good Shepherd, …
Jesus, True Light, …
Jesus, Eternal Wisdom, …
Jesus, Infinite Goodness, …
Jesus, the Way, the Truth, and the Life, …
Jesus, the Joy of angels, …
Jesus, King of patriarchs, …
Jesus, Master of the apostles, …
Jesus, Teacher of the evangelists, …

Jesus, Strength of martyrs, ...

Have mercy on us.

Jesus, Light of confessors, ...

Jesus, Purity of virgins, ...

Jesus, Crown of all saints, ...

Be merciful unto us,   **Spare us, O Jesus.**

Be merciful unto us,   **Hear us, O Jesus.**

From all evil,   **Lord Jesus, deliver us.**

From all sin, ...

From your wrath, ...

From the snares of the devil, ...

From the spirit of fornication, ...

From everlasting death, ...

From a neglect of your holy inspiration, ...

Through the mystery of your holy incarnation, ...

Through your nativity, ...

Through your divine infancy, ...

Through your sacred life, ...

Through your labors and travails, ...

Through your agony and passion, ...

Through your cross and dereliction, ...

Through your pains and torments, ...

Through your death and burial, ...

Through your holy resurrection, ...

Through your admirable ascension, ...

Through the coming of the Holy Spirit, the Comforter, ...

In the day of judgment, ...

Lamb of God, who takes away the sins of the world,   **Spare us, O Lord Jesus.**
Lamb of God, who takes away the sins of the world,   **Hear us, O Lord Jesus.**
Lamb of God, who takes away the sins of the world,   **Have mercy on us, O Lord Jesus.**

Christ Jesus,   **Hear us.**
Christ Jesus,   **Graciously hear us.**

V. May the name of the Lord be blessed.
R. Now, and forever.

Let us pray.

O Lord Jesus Christ, who has said, "Ask, and you shall receive; seek, and you shall find; knock, and it shall be opened unto you," grant, we beseech you, to us your supplicants, the gifts of your divine love, that we may love you with our hearts in word and deed, and never cease from praising you: who lives and reigns, for ever and ever.

O God, who has rendered the most glorious name of your only begotten Son, our Lord Jesus Christ, most worthy to be loved with the highest affection by your faithful, and to be exceedingly dreadful to evil spirits, mercifully grant that all who devoutly honor the sacred name of Jesus on earth may receive in this life the sweetness of holy consolation, and obtain in the future the happi-

ness of eternal joy and bliss: through the same,
Christ, Our Lord.

May the divine assistance always remain with us.
R. Amen.

Litany of the Sacred Heart

Lord, have mercy.	**Lord, have mercy.**
Christ, have mercy.	**Christ, have mercy.**
Lord, have mercy.	**Lord, have mercy.**

God our Father in heaven,   **Have mercy on us.**
God the Son, Redeemer of the world, …
God the Holy Spirit, …
Holy Trinity, one God, …
Heart of Jesus, Son of the eternal Father, …
Heart of Jesus, formed by the Holy Spirit in the
    womb of the Virgin Mother, …
Heart of Jesus, one with the eternal Word, …
Heart of Jesus, infinite in majesty, …
Heart of Jesus, holy temple of God, …
Heart of Jesus, tabernacle of the Most High, …
Heart of Jesus, house of God and gate of
    heaven, …
Heart of Jesus, aflame with love for us, …
Heart of Jesus, source of justice and love, …
Heart of Jesus, full of goodness and love, …
Heart of Jesus, wellspring of all virtue, …
Heart of Jesus, worthy of all praise, …
Heart of Jesus, king and center of all hearts, …

Heart of Jesus, treasure house of wisdom and
    knowledge, ...   **Have mercy on us.**

Heart of Jesus, in whom there dwells the
    fullness of God, ...

Heart of Jesus, in whom the Father is well
    pleased, ...

Heart of Jesus, from whose fullness we have all
    received, ...

Heart of Jesus, desire of the eternal hills, ...

Heart of Jesus, patient and full of mercy, ...

Heart of Jesus, generous to all who turn
    to you, ...

Heart of Jesus, fountain of life and holiness, ...

Heart of Jesus, atonement for our sins, ...

Heart of Jesus, overwhelmed with insults, ...

Heart of Jesus, broken for our sins, ...

Heart of Jesus, obedient even to death, ...

Heart of Jesus, pierced by a lance, ...

Heart of Jesus, source of all consolation, ...

Heart of Jesus, our life and resurrection, ...

Heart of Jesus, our peace and reconciliation, ...

Heart of Jesus, victim for our sins, ...

Heart of Jesus, salvation of all who trust
    in you, ...

Heart of Jesus, hope of all who die in you, ...

Heart of Jesus, delight of all the saints, ...

Lamb of God, you take away the sins of the world.
        Have mercy on us.

Lamb of God, you take away the sins of the world.
Have mercy on us.
Lamb of God, you take away the sins of the world.
Have mercy on us.

V. Jesus, gentle and humble of heart,
R. Touch our hearts and make them like your own.

Let us pray,
Father, we rejoice in the gifts of love we have received from the heart of Jesus, your Son. Open our hearts to share his life and continue to bless us with his love. We ask this in the name of Jesus the Lord.
R. Amen.[1]

Litany of the Blessed Virgin Mary
(Also called the Litany of Loreto)
Lord, have mercy on us.
Christ, have mercy on us.
Lord, have mercy on us. Christ, hear us.
Christ, graciously hear us.

God the Father of heaven, **Have mercy on us.**
God the Son, Redeemer of the world,
Have mercy on us.
God the Holy Spirit, **Have mercy on us.**
Holy Trinity, one God, **Have mercy on us.**

Holy Mary,	**Pray for us.**
Holy Mother of God, ...	
Holy Virgin of virgins, ...	
Mother of Christ, ...	
Mother of the Church, ...	
Mother of divine grace, ...	
Mother most pure, ...	
Mother most chaste, ...	
Mother inviolate, ...	
Mother undefiled, ...	
Mother immaculate, ...	
Mother most amiable, ...	
Mother most admirable, ...	
Mother of good counsel, ...	
Mother of our Creator, ...	
Mother of our Savior, ...	
Virgin most prudent, ...	
Virgin most venerable, ...	
Virgin most renowned, ...	
Virgin most powerful, ...	
Virgin most merciful, ...	
Virgin most faithful, ...	
Mirror of justice, ...	
Seat of wisdom, ...	
Cause of our joy, ...	
Spiritual vessel, ...	
Vessel of honor, ...	
Singular vessel of devotion, ...	
Mystical rose, ...	

Tower of David, ...   **Pray for us.**
Tower of Ivory, ...
House of gold, ...
Ark of the covenant, ...
Gate of heaven, ...
Morning star, ...
Health of the sick, ...
Refuge of sinners, ...
Comforter of the afflicted, ...
Help of Christians, ...
Queen of angels, ...
Queen of patriarchs, ...
Queen of prophets, ...
Queen of apostles, ...
Queen of martyrs, ...
Queen of confessors, ...
Queen of virgins, ...
Queen of all saints, ...
Queen conceived without original sin, ...
Queen assumed into heaven, ...
Queen of the most holy Rosary, ...
Queen of peace, ...

V. Lamb of God, who takes away the sins of
   the world,
R. Spare us, O Lord.
V. Lamb of God, who takes away the sins of
   the world,
R. Graciously hear us, O Lord.

V. Lamb of God, who takes away the sins of the world,
R. Have mercy on us.

V. Pray for us, O holy Mother of God,
R. That we may be made worthy of the promises of Christ.

Let us pray.

O God, whose only begotten Son, by his life, death, and resurrection, has purchased for us the rewards of everlasting life; grant, we beseech you, that we who meditate on these mysteries of the most holy Rosary of the Blessed Virgin Mary, may both imitate what they contain, and obtain what they promise. Through the same, Christ our Lord.
R. Amen.

A pious custom suggests adding the following prayers after the litany:

For the needs of the Church and of the nation:
Our Father. Hail Mary. Glory Be.

For the (arch)bishop of this diocese and his intentions:
Our Father. Hail Mary. Glory Be.

For the holy souls in purgatory:
Our Father. Hail Mary. May they rest in peace.
R. Amen.

Litany of the Saints

When a person is in danger of death, the litany may be prayed for him or her with special mention of the person's patron saint. This litany is also prayed at Easter, baptisms, and ordinations.

Lord, have mercy.	**Lord, have mercy.**
Christ, have mercy.	**Christ, have mercy.**
Lord, have mercy.	**Lord, have mercy.**

Holy Mary, Mother of God, **Pray for him/her.**
Holy angels of God, …
Abraham, our father in faith, …
David, leader of God's people, …
All holy patriarchs and prophets, …
St. John the Baptist, …
St. Joseph, …
St. Peter and St. Paul, …
St. Andrew, …
St. John, …
St. Mary Magdalene, …
St. Stephen, …
St. Ignatius, …
St. Lawrence, …
St. Perpetua and St. Felicity, …
St. Agnes, …
St. Gregory, …
St. Augustine, …
St. Athanasius, …

St. Basil, ...   **Pray for him/her.**
St. Martin, ...
St. Benedict, ...
St. Francis and St. Dominic, ...
St. Francis Xavier, ...
St. John Vianney, ...
St. Catherine, ...
St. Teresa, ...
(Other saints may be included here.)
All holy men and women, ... **Pray for him/her.**

Lord, be merciful,   **Lord, save your people.**
From all evil, ...
From every sin, ...
From Satan's power, ...
At the moment of death, ...
From everlasting death, ...
On the day of judgment, ...
By your coming as man, ...
By your suffering and cross, ...
By your death and rising to new life, ...
By your return in glory to the Father, ...
By your gift of the Holy Spirit, ...
By your coming again in glory, ...

Be merciful to us sinners,
                            Lord, hear our prayer.
Bring N. to eternal life, first promised to him/her
in baptism, ...

Raise N. on the last day, for he/she has eaten the
bread of life, ...   **Lord, hear our prayer.**
Let N. share in your glory, for he/she has shared
in your suffering and death, ...
Jesus, Son of the living God, ...

Christ, hear us.   **Christ, hear us.**
Lord Jesus, hear our prayer.
                        Lord Jesus, hear our prayer.[2]

Litany of St. Joseph

Lord, have mercy.   **Lord, have mercy.**
Christ, have mercy.   **Christ, have mercy.**
Holy Trinity, one God.   **Have mercy on us.**

Holy Mary,   **Pray for us.**
St. Joseph, ...
Noble son of the House of David, ...
Light of patriarchs, ...
Husband of the Mother of God, ...
Guardian of the Virgin, ...
Foster father of the Son of God, ...
Faithful guardian of Christ, ...
Head of the holy family, ...
Joseph, chaste and just, ...
Joseph, prudent and brave, ...
Joseph, obedient and loyal, ...
Pattern of patience, ...
Lover of poverty, ...

Model of workers, ...   **Pray for us.**
Example to parents, ...
Guardian of virgins, ...
Pillar of family life, ...
Comfort of the troubled, ...
Hope of the sick, ...
Patron of the dying, ...
Terror of evil spirits, ...
Protector of the Church, ...

Lamb of God, you take away the sins of the world.
         Have mercy on us.
Lamb of God, you take away the sins of the world.
         Have mercy on us.
Lamb of God, you take away the sins of the world.
         Have mercy on us.

V. God made him master of his household.
R. And put him in charge of all that he owned.

Let us pray.
Almighty God,
in your infinite wisdom and love
you chose Joseph to be the husband of Mary,
the mother of your Son.
As we enjoy his protection on earth,
may we have the help of his prayers in heaven.
We ask this through Christ our Lord.
R. Amen.

NOVENA PRAYERS

A novena is a series of prayers that are prayed over a period of time. The word novena comes from the Latin novenus, *which means a set of nine. Typically, novena prayers are said for nine consecutive days; however, some are said in three or five days, as well as once a week for nine weeks.*

It is believed that novenas originated from the nine days Our Lady and the apostles waited in the upper room between the Ascension of Jesus and the coming of the Holy Spirit on Pentecost. Those who were gathered there spent the time in prayer as they waited.

In addition to praying the prayer or prayers of the novena, the faithful are encouraged to attend daily Mass and Holy Communion, if possible. Novenas can be said publicly in churches or chapels or privately by individuals. Usually a novena is made by invoking the intercession of a particular saint or made directly to God in the hopes of obtaining spiritual or temporal assistance.

"Glory Be to the Father" Novena

By Jesuit Father Putigan (on December 3, 1925)

The "Glory Be to the Father," praising the Holy Trinity, is said 24 times a day for nine days, in thanksgiving for all the blessings and favors given to St. Thérèse of the Child Jesus during the 24 years of her life. In addition, the following or a similar prayer may be used:

> Holy Trinity, God the Father, God the Son, and God the Holy Spirit, I thank You for all the blessings and favors You have showered upon the soul of Your servant Thérèse of the Child Jesus during the 24 years she spent here on earth, and in consideration of the merits of this Your most beloved saint, I beseech You to grant me this favor, if it is in accordance with Your most Holy Will and is not an obstacle to my salvation.

After this prayer should follow the twenty-four Glory Be's, between each of which the following short prayer may be said: "St. Thérèse of the Child Jesus, pray for us."

(While this novena may be said any time, the ninth to the seventeenth of the month is particularly recommended, for on those days the petitioner joins in prayer with others making the novena.)

The Holy Spirit Novena
Prayer of Supplication

Holy Spirit, You who solve all problems, light all roads so that I can obtain my goals, You give me the divine gift to forgive and forget all evils against me, and in all instances of my life You are with me. I want in this short prayer to thank You and to confirm that I never want to be separated from You, even in spite of my material illusions. I wish to be with You in eternal glory. Thank You for Your mercy toward me and mine.

(Recite this prayer for three consecutive days.)

Sacred Heart of Jesus Efficacious Novena
(Prayed daily by Padre Pio)

I. Oh, my Jesus, You said, "Verily I say to you, ask and you shall receive, seek and you shall find, knock and it shall be opened to you," behold I knock, I seek, and I ask for the grace of *(mention your request here).*

   Our Father. Hail Mary. Glory Be. Sacred Heart of Jesus, I put all my trust in You.

II. Oh, my Jesus, You said, "Verily I say to you, whatsoever you shall ask the Father in My name, He will give it to you," behold in your name I ask the Father for the grace of *(mention your request here).*

*Our Father. Hail Mary. Glory Be. Sacred Heart
of Jesus, I put all my trust in You.*

III. Oh, my Jesus, You said, "Verily I say to you,
heaven and earth shall pass away but My words
shall not pass away," behold, encouraged by
your infallible words, I now ask for the grace
of *(mention your request here)*.

*Our Father. Hail Mary. Glory Be. Sacred Heart
of Jesus, I put all my trust in You.*

Oh, Sacred Heart of Jesus, to whom one thing
alone is impossible — namely, not to have compassion on the afflicted — have pity on us miserable
sinners and grant us the grace which we ask of you
through the Sorrowful and Immaculate Heart of
Mary, your and our tender Mother.

(Pray the Hail, Holy Queen)
Hail, holy Queen, Mother of Mercy. Hail, our
life, our sweetness and our hope. To you do we
cry, poor banished children of Eve. To you do we
send up our sighs, mourning, and weeping in this
valley of tears. Turn, then, most gracious advocate,
your eyes of mercy toward us, and after this, our
exile, show unto us the blessed fruit of your womb,
Jesus. O clement, O loving, O sweet Virgin Mary.

(Add this prayer)
St. Joseph, foster father of Jesus, pray for us.

Sacred Heart and Immaculate Heart

May the Sacred Heart of Jesus and the Immaculate Heart of Mary be praised, adored, and glorified every day throughout the world forever.

Amen.

(Pray the above six times a day for nine days.)

Novena for the Missions

Loving Father, to be Christian is to share in the life of God who seeks at every moment to communicate his very self in love. In this way, the Christian life is missionary. Thank you for the witnesses to the Gospel you sent into my life who led me to communion with you. Help me to be an effective missionary and to draw many people into faith-filled friendship with you. Let me communicate to others the reasons for my conversion. May they see in my life of faith an echo of the forgiveness I received. Enable me to overcome any fear or reluctance I have to witness to Jesus Christ.

Bless and protect all foreign missionaries. May the truth of the Gospel be proclaimed to all nations and peoples who do not yet believe in Jesus Christ. United in your Son, I offer my intentions *(mention your request here).*[1]

Thy Most Holy Mother

O Jesus, who has said, "Ask and you will receive, seek and you will find, knock and it shall be opened to you," through the intercession of Mary, Thy Most Holy Mother, I knock, I seek, I ask that my prayers be granted *(mention your request here)*.

O Jesus, who has said, "All you ask of the Father in My Name, He will grant you through the intercession of Mary, My Most Holy Mother," I humbly and urgently ask Thy Father in Thy Name that my prayers be granted *(mention your request here)*.

O Jesus, who has said, "Heaven and earth shall pass, but my word shall not pass," through the intercession of Mary, Thy Most Holy Mother, I feel confident that my prayers will be granted *(mention your request here)*.

(This novena is to be said every hour for nine consecutive hours in one day.)

Blessed Virgin Mary

O most beautiful flower of Mount Carmel, fruitful vine, splendor of Heaven, Blessed Mother of the Son of God, Immaculate Virgin, assist me in this my necessity. O Star of the Sea, help me and show me here you are my Mother. O Holy Mary, Mother of God, Queen of Heaven and Earth, I humbly beseech you from the bottom of my heart to succor me in this necessity. There are none that can withstand your power. O show me herein you are my Mother.

O Mary, conceived without original sin, pray for us who have recourse to thee *(three times)*.

Holy Mother, I place this cause in your hands *(three times)*.

Holy Spirit, You solve all problems. Light all roads so that I can attain my goal. You gave me the divine gift to forgive and forget all evil against me, and in all instances of my life You are with me. I want in this short prayer to thank You for all things as I confirm once again that I never want to be separated from You in eternal glory. Thank You for Your mercy towards me and mine. Amen.

(Recite this prayer for three consecutive days.)

Chaplet of Divine Mercy

By St. Faustina Kowalska

Recite one Our Father, one Hail Mary, and the Apostles' Creed. Then, on the Our Father beads of the rosary, say the following words:

Eternal Father, I offer You the Body and Blood, Soul and Divinity of Your dearly beloved Son, Our Lord Jesus Christ, in atonement for our sins and those of the whole world.

On the Hail Mary beads, say the following words:

For the sake of His sorrowful Passion, have mercy on us and on the whole world.

At the conclusion of each decade, recite three times:

Holy God, Holy Mighty One, Holy Immortal One, have mercy on us and on the whole world.

A Prayer for Divine Mercy
(From the Diary of St. Faustina of the Sisters of Our Lady of Mercy)

O Greatly Merciful God, Infinite Goodness, to-day all mankind calls out from the abyss of its misery to Your mercy — to Your compassion, O God; and it is with its mighty voice of misery that it cries out: Gracious God, do not reject the prayer of this earth's exiles! O Lord, Goodness beyond our understanding, Who are acquainted with our misery through and through, and know that by our power we cannot ascend to You, we implore You, anticipate us with Your grace and keep on increasing Your mercy in us, that we may faithfully do Your holy will all through our life and at death's hour. Let the omnipotence of Your mercy shield us from the darts of our salvation's enemies, that we may with confidence, as Your children, await Your final coming — that day known to You alone. And we expect to obtain everything promised us by Jesus in spite of all our wretchedness. For Jesus is our Hope: Through His merciful Heart as through an open gate we pass through to heaven.[2]

(St. Faustina Kowalska , 1905-1938, was a humble Polish nun who received the message of Divine Mercy in revelations. The Church celebrates Divine Mercy Sunday on the Sunday after Easter, and the chaplet is prayed beginning on the Easter Vigil. It may also be prayed at other times.)

Immaculate Conception

Immaculate Virgin Mary, you were pleasing in the sight of God from the first moment of your conception in the womb of your mother, St. Anne. You were chosen to be the Mother of Jesus Christ, the Son of God. I believe the teaching of Holy Mother the Church, that in the first instant of your conception, by the singular grace and privilege of Almighty God, in virtue of the merits of Jesus Christ, Savior of the human race and your beloved Son, you were preserved from all stain of original sin. I thank God for this wonderful privilege and grace He bestowed upon you as I honor your Immaculate Conception. Look graciously upon me as I implore this special favor *(mention your request here).*

Virgin Immaculate, Mother of God and my Mother, from your throne in heaven turn your eyes of pity upon me. Filled with confidence in your goodness and power, I beg you to help me in this journey of life, which is so full of dangers for my soul. I entrust myself entirely to you, that I may never be the slave of the devil through sin, but may always live a humble and pure life. I consecrate myself to you forever, for my only desire is to love your Divine Son, Jesus. Mary, since none of your devout servants has ever perished, may I, too, be saved. Amen.

(The novena is prayed for nine days, ending on the feast of the Immaculate Conception on December 8.)

Mary, Queen of All Hearts

O Mary, Queen of All Hearts, advocate of the most hopeless cases, Mother most pure, most compassionate, Mother of Divine Love, full of divine light, we confide to your care the favors we ask of you today *(mention your request here).*

Consider our misery, our tears, our interior trials and sufferings. We know that you can help us through the merits of your Divine Son, Jesus. We promise, if our prayers are heard, to spread your glory by making you known under the title Mary, Queen of All Hearts, Queen of the Universe.

Grant, we beseech you, hear our prayers, for every day you give us so many proofs of your love and your power of intercession to heal both body and soul. We hope against all hope. Ask Jesus to cure us, pardon us, and grant us final perseverance.

(Repeat three times) O Mary, Queen of All Hearts, help us. We have confidence in you.

(Recite this prayer for nine consecutive days and receive the sacraments of Penance and Holy Eucharist.)

Our Lady of Good Success

Our Lady, our Queen and our Mother, in the name of Jesus, and for the love of Jesus, we implore thee to take our cause in thy hands and grant it good success. Amen.

(Recite this prayer for nine consecutive days, especially during the months of May and October.)

Our Lady of Grace

Remember, O most amiable Virgin Mary, the ineffable power which the Holy Trinity conferred on you when constituting you the Mother of Grace. Animated with entire confidence in your all-powerful mediation, I place into your blessed hands the needs, the intentions, and the persons of all who are dear to me and for whom I am bound to pray. I pray especially for the exaltation of Holy Mother Church, the acknowledgment of the rights of her august Head, for priests, for the conversion of sinners, the relief of the holy souls in purgatory, and particularly for *(mention your request here)*.

Hail Mary …

Mother of love, of sorrow, and of mercy, pray for us.

(St. Padre Pio of Pietrelcina prayed to Our Lady of Grace every day. Her image was in the San Giovanni Rotondo church, where he lived in Italy. The prayer may also be used as a typical novena prayer for nine days.)

Our Lady of Lourdes

O ever Immaculate Virgin, Mother of mercy, health of the sick, refuge of sinners, comforter of the afflicted, you know my wants, my troubles, my sufferings; look with mercy on me.

By appearing in the Grotto of Lourdes, you were pleased to make it a privileged sanctuary, whence you dispense your favors; and already many sufferers have obtained the cure of their infirmities, both spiritual and corporal.

I come, therefore, with complete confidence to implore your maternal intercession.

Obtain, O loving Mother, the grant of my requests.

Through gratitude for your favors, I will endeavor to imitate your virtues, that I may one day share your glory.

Amen.

(Recite this prayer for nine consecutive days. Our Lady of Lourdes feast day is February 11.)

Our Lady of the Miraculous Medal

O Immaculate Virgin Mary, Mother of our Lord Jesus and our Mother, penetrated with the most lively confidence in your all-powerful and never-failing intercession, manifested so often through the Miraculous Medal, we, your loving and trustful children, implore you to obtain for us the graces and favors we ask during this novena, if they be beneficial to our immortal souls, and the souls for whom we pray *(mention your request here)*.

You know, O Mary, how often our souls have been the sanctuaries of your Son who hates iniquity. Obtain for us then a deep hatred of sin and that purity of heart which will attach us to God alone so that our every thought, word, and deed may tend to His greater glory. Obtain for us also a spirit of prayer and self-denial that we may discover by penance what we have lost by sin and at length attain to that blessed abode where you are Queen of Angels and of men. Amen.

(Recite this prayer for nine consecutive days.)

Prayer to Mary, Undoer of Knots

Holy Mary, full of the presence of God, during your life you accepted with great humility the holy will of the Father and the legacy of your Son, our Lord Jesus Christ, and evil never dared to entangle you with its confusion. Since then you have interceded for all of our difficulties as you did at the wedding feast of Cana. With all simplicity and with patience, you have given us an example of how to untangle the knots in our complicated lives. By being our mother forever, you arrange and make clear the path that unites us to Our Lord.

Holy Mary, Mother of God and ours, with your maternal heart, untie the knots that upset our lives. We ask you to receive into your hands *(mention your prayer request here)* and deliver us from the chains and confusion that restrain us.

Blessed Virgin Mary, through your grace, your intercession, and by your example, deliver us from evil and untie the knots that keep us from being united to God. So that free of all confusion and error, we may find him in all things, keep him in our hearts, and serve him always in our brothers and sisters.

Mother of Good Counsel, pray for us. Amen.[3]

Mary, Undoer of Knots, pray for me.

(Recite this prayer for nine consecutive days.)

—— Saints' Novenas ——

(Note: Unless otherwise indicated, recite the prayer for a saint's novena on nine consecutive days.)

St. Agatha Novenas

Lord God, St. Agatha always pleased you by her chastity and in the end by her martyrdom. May she obtain for us a merciful pardon for our sins and a complete cure for the breast cancer from which I presently suffer.

Amen.

Almighty and eternal God, in Whose Providence all things are, through the intercession of St. Agatha, Virgin and Martyr, we beseech Thee to deliver us from fire and earthquake and from every other evil. We make this prayer through Our Lord Jesus Christ, Your Son, Who lives and reigns with You and the Holy Spirit, One God, forever and ever.

Amen.

(St. Agatha suffered martyrdom in 251 in Sicily when she rejected the advances of the governor. Patron of nurses and also invoked against earthquakes, fire, lightning, and diseases of the breast. Feast: February 5.)

St. Angela Merici

O Lord, shed your light on the dark places of my heart, and grant me the grace rather to die than ever offend your Divine Majesty. Give stability, O Lord, to my affections and sentiments, so that they may cause me to commit no transgression, nor to take my prayers away from the light of your countenance, which is the sweet comfort of every afflicted soul.

(St. Angela Merici, 1474-1540, founded the first teaching order of women, which would become the Ursulines. Patron of the sick, the handicapped, and the disabled, and those who have lost their parents. Feast: January 27.)

St. Anne

Glorious St. Anne, I desire to honor you with a special devotion. I choose you, after the Blessed Virgin, as my spiritual mother and protectress. To you I entrust my soul and my body, all my spiritual and temporal interests, as well as those of my family. To you I consecrate my mind, that in all things it may be enlightened by faith; my heart, that you may keep it pure and fill it with love for Jesus, Mary, Joseph, and yourself; my will, that like yours, it may always be one with the Will of God.

Good St. Anne, filled with love for those who invoke you with compassion for those who suffer,

I confidently place before you my earnest petition *(mention your request here).*

I beg you to recommend my petition to your daughter, the Blessed Virgin Mary, that both Mary and you may present it to Jesus. Through your earnest prayers may my request be granted. But if what I ask should not be according to the Will of God, obtain for me that which will be for the greater benefit of my soul. By the power and the grace with which God has blessed you, extend to me your helping hand.

But most of all, merciful St. Anne, I beg you to help me to master my evil inclinations and temptations, and to avoid all occasions of sin. Obtain for me the grace of never offending God, of fulfilling faithfully all the duties of my state of life, and of practicing all those virtues that are needful for my salvation.

Like you, may I belong to God in life and in death through perfect love. And after having loved and honored you on earth as a truly devoted child, may I, through your prayers, have the privilege of loving and honoring you in heaven with the angels and saints throughout eternity.

Good St. Anne, mother of her who is our life, our sweetness, and our hope, pray to her for me and obtain my request.

Amen.

Glorious and holy St. Anne, whom the Heavens admire, whom the saints honor, and the earth reveres — the just, the penitent, and the sinner consider you as their powerful advocate before God, for by your intercession the just hope for an increase of grace, the penitent for their justification, the sinners for the remission of their sins. Be, then, kind and generous to me. Pray for me in Heaven. Use in my favor the great influence you have before God, particularly for *(mention your request here)*. Obtain my request and grant that I may live always close to God.

Good St. Anne, mother of her who is our life, our sweetness, and our hope, pray to her for me and obtain my request.

(Our Father. Hail Mary. Glory Be.)

(St. Anne, first century B.C., is the mother of Mary, the Blessed Mother, and wife of Joachim. Patron of widows, childless women, pregnant women, nurse-maids, and plague victims. Feast: July 26.)

St. Anthony of Padua Novenas

St. Anthony, glorious for the fame of your miracles, obtain for me from God's mercy this favor that I desire *(mention your request here)*. Since you were so gracious to poor sinners, do not regard my lack of virtue but consider the glory of God which will be exalted once more through you by the granting of the petition that I now earnestly present to you.

Glorious Wonderworker St. Anthony, father of the poor and comforter of the afflicted, I ask for your help. You have come to my aid with such loving care and have comforted me so generously. I offer you my heartfelt thanks. Accept this offering of my devotion and love and with it my earnest promise which I now renew, to live always in the love of God and my neighbor. Continue to shield me graciously with your protection, and obtain for me the grace of being able one day to enter the Kingdom of Heaven, there to praise with you the everlasting mercies of God.

Amen.

O holy St. Anthony, gentlest of saints, your love for God and charity for His creatures made you worthy, when on earth, to possess miraculous powers. Miracles waited on your word, which you were ever ready to speak for those in trouble or anxiety. Encouraged by this thought, I implore of you to obtain for me *(mention your request here)*. The answer to my prayer may require a miracle; even so, you are the Saint of Miracles. O gentle and loving St. Anthony, whose heart was ever full of human sympathy, whisper my petition into the ears of the Sweet Infant Jesus, who loved to be folded in your arms; and the gratitude of my heart will be ever yours.

Amen.

———

Tony, Tony, please come round, something's lost and must be found.

St. Camillus de Lellis

Glorious St. Camillus, you have shown yourself to be a true Father to the Sick and Infirm, and you have been chosen by the Holy Father to be their patron in heaven. Obtain for us, we beseech you, lively faith, submission to the holy Will of God, and the spirit of true repentance. Obtain for us likewise, we implore you, the recovery of our health, especially *(mention your request here)*, if this should be pleasing to Him who loves us.

Amen.

(St. Camillus, 1550-1614, founder of the Ministers of the Sick, was devoted to prayer and service to the sick and the suffering. Patron of the sick, nurses, and caregivers. Feast: July 18.)

St. Edith Stein

Dear Sister Teresa Benedicta of the Cross,
Child of the Day of Atonement — Yom Kippur,
Daughter of Abraham,
Bride of Christ,

Seeker of truth,
Scholar of the Church,
Handmaid of Our Lady of Mount Carmel,
Servant of the Suffering Servant,
Presence of mercy,
Victim of victimizer,
Embracer of the Cross of Christ-like love,
Martyr of Auschwitz,
Imitator of Jesus,
Conqueror of evil,
Friend of God, Edith,
Please pray for me.
Please intercede for this petition of mine
    (mention your petition here).
Amen.

St. Edith Stein, Sister Teresa Benedicta of the Cross, pray for us.

(St. Edith Stein, 1891-1942, was a German Jewish philosopher who converted to Catholicism, becoming a Discalced Carmelite nun. She died a martyr in the concentration camp at Auschwitz. Feast: August 9.)

St. Francis Xavier

The Novena of Grace

O most lovable and loving saint, in union with thee I adore the divine Majesty. My heart is filled with joy at the remembrance of the marvelous favors with which God blessed thy life on earth and of the great glory that came to thee after death. In union with thee I praise God and offer Him my humble tribute of thanksgiving. I implore thee to obtain for me, through thy powerful intercession, the greatest of blessings: that of living and dying in the state of grace. I also beg of thee to secure for me the special favor I ask in this novena *(mention your request here)*. May the will of God be done. If what I am praying for is not for God's glory and for the good of my soul, I beseech thee to obtain for me what is most conducive to this end.

V. Pray for us, St. Francis Xavier.
R. That we may be made worthy of the promises of Christ.

(This novena may be recited from March 4 to 12, in honor of the recovery of a dying priest in 1533. It may also be offered in preparation for the feast of St. Francis Xavier on December 3.)

St. Gertrude the Great

I salute you through the Heart of Jesus, O all you holy angels and saints of God; I rejoice in your glory and I give thanks to Our Lord for all the benefits which He has showered upon you.

I praise Him and glorify Him, and offer you, for an increase of your joy and honor, the most gentle Heart of Jesus. Deign, therefore, to pray for me that I may become according to the heart of God. Amen.

(St. Gertrude the Great, 1256-1302, was a Cistercian nun and mystic who received many private revelations and spread devotion to the Sacred Heart. Feast: November 16.)

St. John Bosco

In need of special help, I appeal with confidence to you, O St. John Bosco, for I require not only spiritual graces but also temporal ones, and particularly *(mention your request here)*. May you, who on earth had such great devotion to Jesus in the Blessed Sacrament, and to Mary, Help of Christians, and who always had compassion for those who were in suffering, obtain from Jesus and from His heavenly Mother the grace I now request, and also a sincere resignation to the Will of God.

St. Joseph Novenas

St. Joseph, you are the faithful protector and intercessor of all who love and venerate you. I have special confidence in you. You are powerful with God and will never abandon your faithful servants. I humbly invoke you and commend myself, with all who are dear to me, to your intercession. By the love you have for Jesus and Mary, do not abandon me during life, and assist me at the hour of my death.

Glorious St. Joseph, spouse of the immaculate Virgin, foster father of Jesus Christ, obtain for me a pure, humble, and charitable mind, and perfect resignation to the Divine Will. Be my guide, my father, and my model through life that I may merit to die as you did in the arms of Jesus and Mary.

Loving St. Joseph, faithful follower of Jesus Christ, I raise my heart to you to implore your powerful intercession in obtaining from the Heart of Jesus all the graces necessary for my spiritual and temporal welfare, particularly the grace of a happy death, and the special grace I now implore *(mention your request here)*. Guardian of the Word Incarnate, I am confident that your prayers on my behalf will be graciously heard before the throne of God.

St. Juan Diego Novena for Migrants

St. Juan Diego, you are our first American indigenous saint.

Please pray that God the Father would protect all migrants through his Son, Jesus Christ.

Ask the Father to pour out the love of the Holy Spirit upon all who are isolated, alone, and separated by choice or necessity from their native lands.

May those torn away from their families and forced to leave their country to find work elsewhere be reunited: husbands with wives and parents with children.

We ask especially for migrant women and children who are particularly vulnerable to the dangers of human trafficking. Give them your protection and shield them from evil.

May we as a Church receive the grace to welcome with love migrants who enter into our country, seeking a home in our parishes and communities.

We ask for your prayers and intercession for all immigrants who are desperate, alone, and in need of God's loving support.

And we ask Our Lady, who appeared to you as your Mother and Mother of all in our land, to wrap her mantle of protection around all migrant people.

We beg for her love, compassion, help, and protection on all immigrants who today experience great sufferings, sorrows, necessities, and misfortunes. Amen.[4]

(St. Juan Diego, 1474-1548, a native Mexican, was asked by Our Lady that a church be built. He received a miraculous image of Our Lady on his tilma [cloak], an image still honored today in the Basilica of Our Lady of Guadalupe, in Mexico City. Feast: December 9.)

St. Jude Novenas

May the Sacred Heart of Jesus be adored, glorified, loved, and preserved throughout the world now and forever. Sacred Heart of Jesus, pray for us. St. Jude, worker of miracles, help to the helpless, pray for us.

(Pray the above novena nine times a day for nine days.)

— —

St. Jude, glorious Apostle, faithful servant, and friend of Jesus: The name of the traitor has caused you to be forgotten by many, but the Church honors and invokes you universally as the patron of difficult and desperate cases. Pray for me, who am so miserable. Make use, I implore you, of that particular privilege accorded to you to bring visible and speedy help where help was almost despaired of. Come to my assistance in this great need that I may receive the consolation and help of heaven in all my necessities, tribulations, and sufferings, particularly *(mention your request here)*, and that I may bless God with you and all the Elect throughout all eternity.

I promise you, O blessed Jude, to be ever mindful of this great favor, and I will never cease to honor you as my special and powerful patron and do all in my power to encourage devotion to you.

St. Jude, pray for us and for all who honor and invoke thy aid.

Pray the Our Father, Hail Mary, and Glory Be three times.

(St. Jude, d. first century, was one of the Twelve Apostles, brother of St. James the Less, martyred with Simon in Persia. Patron of impossible and lost causes. Feast: October 28.)

St. Lucy Novena for Eyes

O God, our Creator and Redeemer, mercifully hear our prayers, and as we venerate Your servant, St. Lucy, for the light of faith You bestowed upon her, increase and preserve this same light also to our souls, that we may be able to avoid evil, to do good, and abhor nothing so much as the blindness and the darkness of evil and of sin.

Relying on Your goodness, O God, we humbly ask You by intercession of Your servant, St. Lucy, to give perfect vision to our eyes, that they may serve for Your greater honor and glory, for our salvation and that of others, and that we may come to the enjoyment of the unfailing light of the Lamb of God in paradise.

St. Lucy, virgin and martyr, hear our prayers and obtain our petitions.

(St. Lucy, d. 304, virgin martyr of Sicily, mentioned in the First Eucharistic Prayer, endured many tortures and is invoked for eye problems. Feast: December 13.)

St. Marianne Cope
Novena for the Poor

Lord Jesus, you who gave us your commandment of love of God and neighbor, and identified yourself in a special way with the most needy of your people, hear our prayer. Faithful to your teaching, St. Marianne Cope loved and served her neighbor, especially the most desolate outcast, giving herself generously and heroically for those afflicted by leprosy. She alleviated their physical and spiritual sufferings, thus helping them to accept their afflictions with patience. Her care and concern for others manifested the great love you have for us. Through her merits and intercession, grant us the favor which we confidently ask of you so that the people of God, following the inspiration of her life and apostolate, may practice charity towards all according to your word and example. Amen.

Through the intercession of St. Marianne Cope, I ask for the grace of *(mention your request here). (Our Father. Hail Mary. Glory Be.)*

(St. Marianne Cope, 1838-1918, known as St. Marianne of Molokai, ministered to the sick, including lepers in Hawaii, and was canonized by Pope Benedict XVI on October 21, 2012. Feast: January 23.)

St. Michael the Archangel

Please protect us, St. Michael the Archangel, against violence, murder, and robbery. In your goodness, preserve us today from all the malice of sinful and wicked men. In your sleepless vigilance, watch over the safety and welfare of our homes, and keep guard over our possessions. Ever hold in your special care, most triumphant St. Michael, the forces of public order against the crimes of evil men, and defend all honest citizens in times of peril. We ask this of you through Christ, our Lord. Amen.

V. Lord, you have given your angels charge of us.
R. To keep us in all our ways.

St. Michael, the Archangel, defend us in battle; be our defense against the wickedness and snares of the devil. May God rebuke him, we humbly pray; and do thou, O Prince of the heavenly host, by the power of God, thrust into hell Satan and the other evil spirits who prowl about the world seeking the ruin of souls.
Amen.

St. Monica Novenas for Conversions

Dear St. Monica, troubled wife and mother, many sorrows pierced your heart during your lifetime.

Yet you never despaired or lost faith. With confidence, persistence, and profound faith, you prayed daily for the conversion of your beloved husband, Patricius, and your beloved son, Augustine.

Grant me that same fortitude, patience, and trust in the Lord. Intercede for me, dear St. Monica, that God may favorably hear my plea for *(mention your request here)* and grant me the grace to accept his will in all things, through Jesus Christ, our Lord, in the unity of the Holy Spirit, one God forever and ever.

Amen.

Daily Novena Prayer to St. Monica

Remember, dear St. Monica, the joy that flooded your heart when Augustine, the son of your prayers and tears, turned his life over to the Lord.

Please present our novena petitions before God, in whose presence you stand. Obtain for us, if it be His holy will, the graces we request through your intercessory power, that we may experience the happiness of answered prayer.

Amen.

(St. Monica, 332-387, born in North Africa, was the mother of St. Augustine. She prayed many years for the conversion of her son and was finally successful. Patron of married women and Christian mothers. Feast: August 27.)

St. Odilia Novena for Eye Problems

O God, Who in Your kindness did give us St. Odilia, Virgin and Martyr, as the Protectress of the eyes and afflicted, grant us, we humbly beseech You, to be protected, through her intercession, from the darkness of ignorance and sin and to be cured from the blindness of the eyes and other bodily infirmities. Through Him, Who is the Light and Life of the world, Jesus Christ, Your Son, Our Lord. Amen.

(St. Odilia, d.c. 720, born in Alsace, was miraculously cured of blindness at age 12. She is invoked for those with afflictions of the eyes. Feast: December 13.)

St. Padre Pio of Pietrelcina
Novena for Healing

Beloved Padre Pio,

Today I come to add my prayer to the thousands of prayers offered to you every day by those who love and venerate you. They ask for cures and healings, earthly and spiritual blessings, and peace for body and mind. And because of your friendship with the Lord, he heals those you ask to be healed, and forgives those you forgive.

Through your visible wounds of the Cross, which you bore for fifty years, you were chosen in our time to glorify the crucified Jesus. Because the Cross has been replaced by other symbols, please help us to bring it back in our midst, for we acknowledge it is the only true sign of salvation.

As we lovingly recall the wounds that pierced your hands, feet, and side, we not only remember the blood you shed in pain, but your smile, and the invisible halo of sweet-smelling flowers that surrounded your presence, the perfume of sanctity.

Padre Pio, may the healings of the sick become the testimony that the Lord has invited you to join the holy company of Saints. In your kindness, please help me with my own special request *(mention your request here and make the Sign of the Cross)*.

Bless me and my loved ones. In the name of the Father, the Son, and the Holy Spirit.

Amen.

St. Peregrine Novena for Cancer Sufferers

St. Peregrine, whom Holy Mother Church has declared patron of those suffering from running sores and cancer, I confidently turn to you for aid in my present need *(mention your request here)*.

Lest I lose confidence, I beg your kind intercession. Plead with Mary, the Mother of Sorrows, whom you loved so tenderly and in union with whom you have suffered the pains of cancer, that she may help me with her all-powerful prayers and consolation.

Obtain for me the strength to accept my trials

from the loving hand of God with patience and resignation. May suffering lead me to a better life and enable me to atone for my own sins and the sins of the world.

St. Peregrine, help me to imitate you in bearing whatever cross God may permit to come to me, uniting myself with Jesus Crucified and the Mother of Sorrows. I offer my sufferings to God with all the love of my heart, for His glory and the salvation of souls, especially my own.

Amen.

(St. Peregrine, 1260-1345, Italian, was received into the Order of the Servants of Mary. Cancer in his foot was cured the night before he was scheduled to have it amputated. He is the patron saint of cancer patients and those suffering from running sores. Feast: May 2.)

St. Peter Novena Prayer for the Forgiveness of Sins

Blessed Apostle Peter, to whom God has given the keys of the kingdom of Heaven and the power to bind and loose, grant that we may be delivered through the help of your intercession from the bonds of our sins.

O Holy Shepherd, Prince of the Apostles, pray for us that we may be made worthy of the promises of Christ.

(Jesus made the fisherman Peter the chief of the apostles and head of the Church, the first pope. St. Peter was martyred by crucifixion in 64 or 65. Feast: June 29.)

Prayer for the Beatification of Venerable Solanus Casey

O God, I adore You. I give myself to You.
May I be the person You want me to be,
and may Your will be done in my life today.

I thank You for the gifts You gave to Father
Solanus. If it is Your Will, bless us with the
beatification of Venerable Solanus so that
others may imitate and carry on his love
for all the poor and suffering of our world.

As he joyfully accepted Your divine plans,
I ask You, according to Your Will, to hear
my prayer for *(mention your request here)*,
through Jesus Christ our Lord. Amen.[5]

(Father Solanus Casey, 1870-1957, an American Capuchin friar, had many miracles attributed to him. Pope St. John Paul II named him Venerable on July 11, 1995. Feast: November 3.)

St. Rita Novena Prayers

Holy Patroness of those in need, St. Rita, so humble, pure and patient, whose pleadings with your

Divine Spouse are irresistible, obtain for us from your crucified Jesus our request *(mention your request here)*. Be favorable towards us for the greater glory of God and yourself, and we promise to honor and sing your praises ever afterward. Amen.

Pray each three times: Our Father, Hail Mary, and Glory Be.

O holy protectress of those who are in utmost need, who shines as a star of hope in the midst of darkness, glorious and blessed St. Rita, bright mirror of the Catholic Church, in patience and fortitude as the patriarch Job, scourge of devils, health of the sick, deliverer of those in extreme need, admiration of saints and model of all states; with my whole heart and soul, prostrate before and firmly united to the adorable will of my God, through the merits of my only Lord and Savior Jesus Christ, and in particular of the merits of His wearing of the torturing crown of thorns, which you with a tender devotion did daily contemplate, through the merits of the most sweet Virgin Mary and your own excellent graces and virtues, I implore you to obtain my earnest petition — provided it be for the greater honor and glory of God and my own sanctification *(mention your request here)*. Do guide and purify my intention, O holy protectress and most dear advocate, that I may obtain the pardon of all my sins, and grace to persevere daily as you did in walking with courage and generosity and unwavering fidelity through the heavenward path in which the love of my sweet Lord desires to lead me. Amen.

—◆—

St. Rita, Advocate of the Hopeless,

Pray for us.

St. Rita, Advocate of the Impossible,

Pray for us.

Pray three Our Fathers, three Hail Marys, and three Glory Be's.

(St. Rita, d. 1457, Italian wife and mother who became a nun upon the death of her husband and two sons, received the wounds of the Crown of Thorns and many visions. Along with St. Jude, she is patron of hopeless cases. Feast: May 22.)

St. Thérèse of Lisieux Novenas

Five-Day Novena

St. Thérèse the Little Flower, please pick me a rose from the heavenly garden and send it to me with a message of love.

Ask God to grant me the favor I implore.

And tell Him I will love Him daily more and more.

Pray five Hail Marys, five Our Fathers, and five Glory Be's.

(If possible, the prayers should be said before 11 a.m. so there is a communion of those praying at the same time.)

Invocation to St. Thérèse

O Glorious St. Thérèse, whom Almighty God has raised up to aid and inspire the human family, I implore your miraculous intercession. You are so powerful in obtaining every need of body and spirit from the Heart of God. Holy Mother Church proclaims you "Prodigy of Miracles … the Greatest Saint of Modern Times." Now I fervently beseech you to answer my petition *(mention your request here)* and to carry out your promises of spending Heaven doing good on earth … of letting fall from Heaven a Shower of Roses.

Little Flower, give me your childlike faith to see the face of God in the people and experiences of my life and to love God with full confidence. St. Thérèse, my Carmelite Sister, I will fulfill your plea "to be made known everywhere" and I will continue to lead others to Jesus through you.

Amen.

(St. Thérèse of the Child Jesus, who died at age 24, promised that "after my death I will let fall a shower of roses." Those who pray for her intercession sometimes receive signs of roses.)

In Thanksgiving for a Favor Received

Thank You, O God, for hearing my prayer and granting my request. Thank You for all the kindness you have shown me.

Thank You, Father, for Your great love in giving me my life, for Your great patience in preserving me despite my sinfulness, for Your protection in the past and for the opportunity to serve and honor You in the future.

Thank You, Lord Jesus, for keeping me numberless times from sin and death by the toils of Your life, the sufferings of Your Passion, and by Your victorious Resurrection.

Thank You, Holy Spirit of God, for bestowing so many graces upon my soul and for having so frequently renewed Your life within me.

May my life, from now on, be a sign of my gratefulness.

Amen.

MASS

The Importance of Mass

Christ Himself instituted the Eucharist at the Last Supper "in order to perpetuate the sacrifice of the Cross throughout the ages until He should come again, and so to entrust to His beloved Spouse, the Church, a memorial of His death and resurrection; a sacrament of love, a sign of unity, a bond of charity, a paschal banquet in which Christ is consumed, the mind is filled with grace, and a pledge of future glory is given to us" (Sacrosanctum Concilium, n. 7, the Constitution on the Sacred Liturgy). *See also Matthew 26:26-28; Mark 14:22-24; Luke 22:17-20; 1 Corinthians 11:23-25.*

Prayer During the Communion Fast

By St. Thomas Aquinas

How holy this feast
in which Christ is our food:
his passion is recalled,
grace fills our hearts,
and we receive a pledge of the glory to come.[1]

Prayer When Taking Holy Water

By this holy water and by your Precious Blood, wash away all my sins, O Lord.

Genuflecting

Upon entering or leaving the pew, bend the right knee to the floor while facing the tabernacle as a sign of reverence to the Real Presence of Jesus in the consecrated Hosts. You may also make the Sign of the Cross as you are genuflecting.

—— PRAYERS BEFORE MASS ——

PRAYERS BY ST. THOMAS AQUINAS

The Physician of Life

Almighty and ever-living God, I draw near to the sacrament of your only begotten Son, our Lord Jesus Christ.

I come sick to the physician of life, unclean to the fountain of mercy, blind to the light of eternal brightness, poor and needy to the Lord of heaven and earth.

So I ask you, most generous Lord: graciously heal my infirmity, wash me clean, illumine my blindness, enrich my poverty, and clothe my nakedness.

May I receive the Bread of angels, the King of kings and Lord of lords, with such reverence and humility, such contrition and devotion, such purity and faith, and such resolve and determination as may secure my soul's salvation.

Grant as I may receive not only the visible sign of the Lord's Body and Blood, but also all the reality and power of the sacrament.

Grant, most kind God, that I may receive the Body of your only begotten Son, our Lord Jesus Christ, which he received from the Virgin Mary, and may receive it in such a way that I become a living part of his Mystical Body and counted among his members.

O most loving Father, grant me your beloved Son. While on this earthly pilgrimage, I receive him under the veil of this sacrament; so may I at last to see him face-to-face for all eternity. For he lives and reigns with you forever and ever.

Amen.

O Sacred Banquet

O Sacred Banquet,
in which Christ is received,
the memory of his passion is renewed,
the soul is filled with grace,
and a pledge of future glory is given to us.

Pange Lingua (Eucharistic Hymn)

Sing, my tongue, the Savior's glory,
Of his Flesh the mystery sing;
Of the Blood, all price exceeding,

Shed by our immortal King,
Destined for the world's redemption,

From a noble womb to spring.
Of a pure and spotless Virgin
Born for us on earth below,
He, as man, with man conversing,
Stayed, the seeds of truth to sow;
Then he closed the solemn order
Wondrously his life of woe.

On the night of that Last Supper,
Seated with his chosen band,
He, the Pascal Victim eating,
First fulfills the Law's command;
Then as Food to all his brethren
Gives himself with his own hand.

Word made flesh, the bread of nature
By his word to Flesh he turns;
Wine into his Blood he changes;
What though sense no change discerns?
Only be the heart in earnest,
Faith her lesson quickly learns.

Tantum Ergo

Down in adoration falling,
Lo! the Sacred Host we hail;
Lo! o'er ancient forms departing,
Newer rites of grace prevail;

Faith for all defects supplying
Where the feeble senses fail.

To the everlasting Father,
And the Son who reigns on high,
With the Holy Spirit proceeding
Forth from each eternally,
Be salvation, honor, blessing,
Might, and endless majesty.
Amen.

(The Pange Lingua *is said to be the greatest of all Eucharistic hymns. The final two verses, the* Tantum Ergo, *are used regularly at Eucharistic adoration.)*

MORE PRAYERS BEFORE MASS

Prayer for the Promotion of Daily Communion

O sweet Jesus, Who did come into this world to enrich the souls of all mankind with the life of Your grace, and Who, to preserve and sustain this life in them, does daily give Thyself in the most august sacrament of the Eucharist as a saving Medicine to heal their infirmities and a Divine Food to support their weakness, we pray and beseech Thee to pour forth upon them most graciously Your Holy Spirit, so that, being filled therewith, any who are in mortal sin may by returning to Thee be restored to the life of grace which they have lost; and that those, who by Your great mercy already serve Thee, may daily, as far as each one is able, come devoutly to Your heavenly banquet and in the strength thereof may find a remedy for their daily venial faults and a support of the life of Your grace and, thus becoming more and more cleansed from sin, may obtain the everlasting happiness of heaven.

Amen.

Assurance of Padre Pio

You must never fail to approach the holy Banquet of the divine Lamb, as nothing will better gather your spirit than its King…. There is no remedy more powerful than this.

Ah, Father, I cannot ask you to remove Jesus from among us … how could I who am so weak and half-hearted live without this Eucharistic food? How could I fulfill that petition made by your Son in our name, "Your will be done, on earth as it is in heaven," if I did not receive strength from this immaculate flesh?

We must always have courage, and if some spiritual languor comes upon us, let us run to the feet of Jesus in the Blessed Sacrament, and let us place ourselves in the midst of the heavenly perfumes, and we will undoubtedly regain our strength.[2]

—— Prayers from the Mass——

The Sign of the Cross

In the name of the Father,
and of the Son,
and of the Holy Spirit.
Amen.

Confiteor

I confess to almighty God
and to you, my brothers and sisters,
that I have greatly sinned,
in my thoughts and in my words,
in what I have done and in what I have failed
     to do,
(And striking their breast, they say:)
through my fault, through my fault,
through my most grievous fault;
therefore I ask blessed Mary ever-Virgin,
all the Angels and Saints,
and you, my brothers and sisters,
to pray for me to the Lord our God.[3]

Kyrie

Lord, have mercy.	*Kyrie, eléison.*
Christ, have mercy.	*Christe, eléison.*
Lord, have mercy.	*Kyrie, eléison.*

Gloria

Glory to God in the highest,
and on earth peace to people of good will.

We praise you,
we bless you,
we adore you,
we glorify you,
we give you thanks for your great glory,
Lord God, heavenly King,
O God, almighty Father.

Lord Jesus Christ, Only Begotten Son,
Lord God, Lamb of God, Son of the Father,
you take away the sins of the world,
    have mercy on us;
you take away the sins of the world,
    receive our prayer;
you are seated at the right hand of the Father,
    have mercy on us.

For you alone are the Holy One,
you alone are the Lord,
you alone are the Most High,
Jesus Christ,
with the Holy Spirit,
in the glory of God the Father.
Amen.[4]

Profession of Faith (Nicene Creed)

I believe in one God,
the Father almighty,
maker of heaven and earth,
of all things visible and invisible.

I believe in one Lord Jesus Christ,
the Only Begotten Son of God,
born of the Father before all ages.
God from God, Light from Light,
true God from true God,
begotten, not made, consubstantial with the
      Father;
through him all things were made.
For us men and for our salvation
he came down from heaven,
and by the Holy Spirit was incarnate of the
      Virgin Mary, and became man.

For our sake he was crucified under Pontius
      Pilate,
he suffered death and was buried,
and rose again on the third day
in accordance with the Scriptures.
He ascended into heaven
and is seated at the right hand of the Father.
He will come again in glory
to judge the living and the dead
and his kingdom will have no end.

I believe in the Holy Spirit, the Lord, the giver
   of life,
who proceeds from the Father and the Son,
who with the Father and the Son is adored
    and glorified,
who has spoken through the prophets.

I believe in one, holy, catholic and apostolic
   Church.
I confess one Baptism for the forgiveness of sins
and I look forward to the resurrection of the dead
and the life of the world to come. Amen.[5]

Sanctus

Holy, Holy, Holy Lord God of hosts.
Heaven and earth are full of your glory.
Hosanna in the highest.
Blessed is he who comes in the name of the Lord.
Hosanna in the highest.[6]

The Lord's Prayer

Our Father, who art in heaven,
hallowed be thy name;
thy kingdom come,
thy will be done
on earth as it is in heaven.
Give us this day our daily bread,
and forgive us our trespasses,
as we forgive those who trespass against us;
and lead us not into temptation,

but deliver us from evil.
Amen.

Lamb of God

Lamb of God, you take away the sins of the
   world, have mercy on us.
Lamb of God, you take away the sins of the
   world, have mercy on us.
Lamb of God, you take away the sins of the
   world, grant us peace.[7]

Lord, I Am Not Worthy

Lord, I am not worthy
that you should enter under my roof,
but only say the word
and my soul shall be healed.[8]

Personal Prayer after Communion

Behold, O kind and most sweet Jesus, I cast myself
on my knees in your sight, and with the most fervent desire of my soul, I pray and beseech you to
impress upon my heart lively sentiments of faith,
hope, and charity, with true repentance for my
sins, and a firm desire of amendment, while with
deep affection and grief of soul I ponder and contemplate your five most precious wounds, having
before my eyes that which David spoke in prophecy: "They pierced My hands and My feet; they
have numbered all My bones."

─────── PRAYERS AFTER MASS ───────

Anima Christi
(Soul of Christ)

Soul of Christ, sanctify me;
Body of Christ, save me;
Blood of Christ, drench me;
Water from the side of Christ, wash me.
Passion of Christ, strengthen me.
O good Jesus, hear me;
Within your wounds hide me;
Never permit me to be separated from you;
From the wicked enemy defend me;
In the hour of my death call me
And bid me come to your side,
That with your saints I may praise you,
For ever and ever.
Amen.

(Attributed by some to Bl. Bernadine of Feltre, 1439-1494. Feast day: September 28.)

Prayer to Christ Crucified

Look down upon me,
good and gentle Jesus,
while before your face I humbly kneel.
and with burning affection
I pray and beg you to fix deep in my heart
lively sentiments of faith, hope, and love,
true contrition for my sins,

and a firm purpose of amendment.
I contemplate with great love and pity
your five most precious wounds,
pondering over them within me,
while I call to mind
the words which David the prophet
said concerning you, my Jesus:
They have pierced my hands and my feet;
they have numbered all my bones.

Prayer After Mass by
St. Thomas Aquinas

Lord, Father all-powerful and ever-living God, I
thank you, for even though I am a sinner, your
unprofitable servant, not because of my worth but
in the kindness of your mercy you have fed me
with the precious Body and Blood of your Son,
our Lord Jesus Christ.

I pray that this Holy Communion may not
bring me condemnation and punishment, but
forgiveness and salvation.

May it be a helmet of faith and a shield of
goodwill.

May it purify me from evil ways and put an
end to my evil passions.

May it bring me charity and patience, humility
and obedience, and growth in the power to do
good.

May it be my strong defense against all my enemies, visible and invisible, and the perfect calming of all my evil impulses, bodily and spiritual.

May it unite me more closely to you, the one true God, and lead me safely through death to everlasting happiness with you.

And I pray that you will lead me, a sinner, to the banquet where you, with your Son and Holy Spirit, are true and perfect light, total fulfillment, everlasting joy, gladness without end, and perfect happiness to your saints.

Grant this through Christ our Lord.

Amen.

Universal Prayer by Pope Clement XI

Lord, I believe in you: increase my faith.

I worship you as my first beginning,
   I long for you as my last end.
   I praise you as my constant helper,
      and call on you as my loving protector.

Guide me by your wisdom,
   correct me with your justice,
   comfort me with your mercy,
   protect me with your power.

I offer you, Lord,
   my thoughts: to be fixed on you;
   my words: to have you for their theme;
   my actions: to reflect my love for you;

my sufferings: to be endured for your greater
glory.

I want to do what you ask of me:
in the way you ask,
for as long as you ask,
because you ask it.

Lord, enlighten my understanding,
strengthen my will,
purify my heart,
and make me holy.

Help me to repent of my past sins
and to resist temptation in the future.
Help me to rise above my human weaknesses
and to grow stronger as a Christian.

Let me love you, my Lord and my God,
to see myself as I really am:
a pilgrim in this world,
a Christian called to respect and love
all those whose lives I touch,
those in authority over me,
my friends and my enemies.

Help me to conquer anger with gentleness,
greed by generosity,
apathy by fervor.
Help me to forget myself and reach out to
others.

Make me prudent in planning,
   courageous in taking risks,
   patient in suffering,
   unassuming in prosperity.

Keep me, Lord, attentive at prayer,
   temperate in food and drink,
   diligent in my work,
   and firm in my intentions.

Let my conscience be clear,
   my conduct without fault,
   my speech blameless,
   my life well-ordered.

Put me on guard against my human weaknesses.
   Let me cherish your love for me,
   keep your law,
   and come at last to your salvation.

Teach me to be aware that this world is passing,
   that my true future is the happiness of
      heaven,
   that life on earth is short,
   and the life to come eternal.

Help me to prepare for death with a proper fear
      of judgment,
   but a greater trust in your goodness.
   Lead me safely through death
   to the endless joys of heaven.

Grant this through Christ our Lord.
Amen.[9]

(Reigning from 1700 to 1721, Pope Clement XI worked for peace, encouraged missionary activity, and had a reputation as a scholarly and holy man.)

EUCHARISTIC ADORATION

During this devotion, the Sacred Host is taken from the tabernacle and placed in a monstrance so it can be seen and venerated by the faithful. Those partaking of this devotion may sit or kneel and silently pray or meditate before the Eucharist.

O Sacrament most holy, O Sacrament divine!
All praise and all thanksgiving be every moment
Thine!

Short Visit to the Blessed Sacrament

By Bl. John Henry Newman

I place myself in the presence of Him, in whose Incarnate Presence I am before I place myself there.

I adore You, O my Savior, present here as God and man, in soul and body, in true flesh and blood.

I acknowledge and confess that I kneel before the Sacred Humanity, which was conceived in Mary's womb, and lay in Mary's bosom; which grew up to man's estate, and by the Sea of Galilee called the Twelve, wrought miracles, and spoke words of wisdom and peace; which in due season hung on the cross, lay in the tomb, rose from the dead, and now reigns in heaven.

I praise and bless, and give myself wholly to Him, Who is the true Bread of my soul, and my everlasting joy.

Before the Blessed Sacrament

(Prayer from the Fátima Children)

O most Holy Trinity, Father, Son, and Holy Spirit, I adore you profoundly. I offer you the most precious body, blood, soul, and divinity of Jesus Christ, present in all the tabernacles of the world, in reparation for the outrages, sacrileges, and indifferences by which He is offended. By the infinite merits of the Sacred Heart of Jesus and the Immaculate Heart of Mary, I beg the conversion of sinners.

(In 1917, Our Lady appeared to three children: ten-year-old Lúcia dos Santos and her cousins, nine-year-old Bl. Francisco and seven-year-old Bl. Jacinta Marto at Fátima, Portugal.)

Prayer of St. Peter Julian Eymard

Oh! Yes, Lord Jesus, come and reign! Let my body be Your temple, my heart Your throne, my will Your devoted servant; let me be Yours forever, living only in You and for you!

(St. Peter Julian Eymard, 1811-1868, a French priest, founded the Blessed Sacrament Fathers and Brothers, dedicated to devotion of the Eucharist. Feast: August 2)

Act When Visiting the Most Holy Sacrament

By St. Alphonsus Liguori

My Lord Jesus Christ, who, for the love you bear to mankind, do remain night and day in this Sacrament, full of pity and love, awaiting, calling, and receiving all who come to visit you; I believe that you are present in the Sacrament of the Altar; I adore you from the depths of my own nothingness; I thank you for the many graces you have given me, and especially for having given me yourself in this Sacrament; for having given me Mary your Mother as my advocate, and for having called me to visit you in this church.

PRAYERS THROUGHOUT THE DAY

It is good to pray for the coming of God's kingdom, but, as the Catechism of the Catholic Church *reminds us, "it is just as important to bring the help of prayer into humble, everyday situations" (CCC 2660).*

—— MORNING PRAYERS ——

(Note: Basic prayers may be used, including the Our Father, Hail Mary, Glory Be, Acts of Faith, Hope and Charity, and the Apostles' Creed.)

Morning Offering

O Jesus, through the Immaculate Heart of Mary, I offer you all my prayers, works, joys, and sufferings of this day, for all the intentions of your Sacred Heart, in union with the Holy Sacrifice of the Mass throughout the world, in reparation for my sins, for the intentions of all my relatives and friends and in particular for the intentions of the Holy Father.

Daily Intentions

These intentions may be used following the Morning Offering:

Sunday: To obtain a true spirit of zeal, religion, and piety. For the success of priests' work and the spiritual welfare of those entrusted to their care.

Monday: Spirit of meekness and humility. Souls in purgatory and religious communities.

Tuesday: Spirit of Faith. Relatives, friends, and benefactors.

Wednesday: Spirit of Charity. The sick, dying, suffering, poor, and those who care for them.

Thursday: Love of the Holy Eucharist. Vocations to the priesthood; conversion of unbelievers; needs of missionaries.

Friday: Spirit of mortification and self-sacrifice. Conversion of sinners.

Saturday: Love of chastity and of the Blessed Virgin. Schools and teachers; children and youth. *(Add your own private intentions to those suggested above.)*[1]

Prayer of Abandonment to God

By Bl. Charles de Foucauld

Father,
I abandon myself into your hands;
do with me what you will.
Whatever you may do, I thank you:
I am ready for all, I accept all.

Let only your will be done in me,
and in all your creatures —
I wish no more than this, O Lord.

Into your hands I commend my soul:
I offer it to you with all the love of my heart,
for I love you, Lord, and so need to give myself,
to surrender myself into your hands without
     reserve,
and with boundless confidence,
for you are my Father.

(Bl. Charles de Foucauld, 1858-1916, French priest murdered in Algeria, was responsible for a number of religious communities and secular institutes for laity and religious. Feast: December 1.)

The *Benedictus*
(Canticle of Zechariah)

(Luke 1:68-79)

Blessed be the Lord, the God of Israel;
he has come to his people and set them free.

He has raised up for us a mighty savior,
born of the house of his servant David.

Through his holy prophets he promised of old
   that he would save us from our enemies,
   from the hands of all who hate us.

He promised to show mercy to our fathers
and to remember his holy covenant.

This was the oath he swore to our father
   Abraham:
to set us free from the hands of our enemies,
free to worship him without fear,
holy and righteous in his sight
   all the days of our life.

You, my child, shall be called the prophet of the
   Most High;
for you will go before the Lord to prepare his
   way,
to give his people knowledge of salvation
by the forgiveness of their sins.

In the tender compassion of our God
the dawn from on high shall break upon us,
to shine on those who dwell in darkness and the
    shadow of death,
and to guide our feet into the way of peace.[2]

(The Church prays this canticle every morning in the Liturgy of the Hours.)

A Morning Prayer

O Jesus,
I offer you my prayers, works, joys, and
    sufferings of this day.
I join myself to all your people,
in praying for the salvation of souls,
    the reunion of all Christians,
        the grace of repentance,
            and the intentions of our Holy Father.
I wish to make my life this day
    a prayer on behalf of _____.
Amen.

A Morning or Evening Prayer

Lord Jesus, I give you my hands to do your work. I give you my feet to go your way. I give you my eyes to see as you see. I give you my tongue to speak your words. I give you my mind to think as you think. I give you my spirit so that you may pray in me. I give you my self so that you may grow in me. So that it is you, Lord Jesus, who lives and works and prays in me. Amen.[3]

Prayer for Sunday Morning

(Psalm 92:1-5)

It is good to give thanks to the LORD,
to sing praises to your name, O Most High;
to declare your steadfast love in the morning,
    and your faithfulness by night,
to the music of the lute and the harp,
    to the melody of the lyre.
For you, O LORD, have made me glad by your
    work
    at the works of your hands I sing for joy.

How great are your works, O LORD! (RSV-SCE)

—— PRAYERS DURING THE DAY——

(Note: Other prayers to use include: the Memorare, *page 35; Hail, Holy Queen, page 36; St. Michael the Archangel, page 89; the Rosary, page 40; and the Chaplet of Divine Mercy, page 113.)*

A Prayer for Today

This is the beginning of a new day. God has given me this day to use as I will. I can waste it — or use it for good, but what I do today is important, because I am exchanging a day of my life for it.

When tomorrow comes, this day will be gone forever, leaving in its place something I have traded for it. I want it to be a gain, and not a loss, and not evil; success, and not failure, in order that I shall not regret the price I have paid for it.[4]

Guardian Angel Prayer

Angel of God,
my guardian dear,
to whom God's love commits me here,
ever this day (night) be at my side,
to light and guard, to rule and guide.
Amen.

Aspirations

These are short prayers that may be said throughout the day to raise ordinary actions to God:

- Lord, help me.
- Jesus, mercy!
- Jesus, I love You.
- O God, have mercy on me, a sinner.
- All for You, most Sacred Heart of Jesus.
- O Lord, increase my faith.
- Glory to the Father, and to the Son, and to the Holy Spirit.
- O God, come to my assistance / O Lord, make haste to help me.

- May the Virgin Mary mild / bless us with her holy Child.
- This is the day the Lord has made / let us be glad and rejoice in it.
- I can do all things in Him who strengthens me.
- I place all my trust in You, O God / all my hope is in Your mercy.
- O Lord, open my lips / and my mouth will proclaim Your praise.
- Gladden the soul of Your servant / for to You, O Lord, I lift up my soul.
- May our radiant Christ lead us from earth to heaven / from death to life.
- We adore You, O Christ, and we bless You / for by Your holy cross You have redeemed the world.

The Jesus Prayer

From early Christian monasticism, simple but intense meditation was encouraged. It consists of repeating one of the following from Scripture or similar forms over and over:

- Jesus Christ, Son of God, have mercy on us!
- Lord Jesus, Son of the living God, have mercy on me a sinner!
- Lord Jesus Christ, have mercy on me, a sinner!

The Angelus

V. The angel of the Lord declared unto Mary;
R. And she conceived by the Holy Spirit.
Hail, Mary ...

V. Behold the handmaid of the Lord.
R. Be it done unto me according to your word.
Hail, Mary ...

V. And the Word was made flesh,
R. And dwelt among us.
Hail, Mary ...

V. Pray for us, O holy Mother of God,
R. That we may be made worthy of the promises of Christ.

Let us pray: Pour forth, we beseech you, O Lord, your grace into our hearts, that we, to whom the incarnation of Christ, your Son, was made known by the message of an angel, may by his passion and cross be brought to the glory of his resurrection, through the same Christ our Lord.

R. Amen.

(The Angelus is traditionally prayed in the early morning, at noon, and in the evening by the faithful who stop to pray.)

—— Mealtime Prayers ——

Grace Before Meals

Bless us, O Lord, and these your gifts
   which we are about to receive
   from your bounty.
Through Christ Our Lord.
Amen.

Many people who have lost a loved one add the following verse:

May the souls of the faithful departed,
through the mercy of God,
rest in peace.
Amen.

Grace at Table

God of all goodness,
through the breaking of bread together
you strengthen the bonds that unite us in love.
Bless ✠ us and these your gifts.
Grant that as we sit down together at table in
   joy and sincerity,
we may grow always closer in the bonds of love.

We ask this through Christ our Lord.
R. Amen.

May your gifts refresh us, O Lord,
and your grace give us strength.
R. Amen.[5]

Thanksgiving After a Meal

We give you thanks, O Lord,
for all the graces and benefits
we have received from your bounty.
Through Christ our Lord.
Amen.

EVENING AND NIGHT PRAYERS

Prayer at Coming Home Each Day

Hear us, Lord,
and send your angel from heaven
to visit and protect,
to comfort and defend
all who live in this house.[6]

The *Magnificat* (Canticle of Mary)

(Luke 1:46-55)

My soul proclaims the greatness of the Lord,
my spirit rejoices in God my Savior
for he has looked with favor on his lowly
    servant.

From this day all generations will call me
  blessed:
The Almighty has done great things for me,
and holy is His Name.

He has mercy on those who fear him
in every generation.

He has shown the strength of his arm,
He has scattered the proud in their conceit.

He has cast down the mighty from their
  thrones,
and has lifted up the lowly.

He has filled the hungry with good things,
and the rich he has sent away empty.

He has come to the help of his servant Israel
for he has remembered his promise of mercy,
the promise he made to our fathers,
to Abraham and his children for ever.[7]

*(The Church prays this canticle every evening in the
Liturgy of the Hours.)*

Prayer in the Evening

By St. Augustine

Watch, O Lord, with those who wake, or watch,
   or weep tonight, and give Your angels and
   saints charge over those who sleep.
   Tend Your sick ones, O Lord Christ;
   Rest Your weary ones; Bless Your dying ones:
   Soothe Your suffering ones;
   Pity Your afflicted ones;
   Shield Your joyous ones;
   And all for Your love's sake.
Amen.

Evening Prayer to Our Blessed Mother

Night is falling, dear Mother, the long day is
   o'er.
And before your loved image I'm kneeling once
   more.
To thank you for keeping me safe thro' the day.
To ask you this night to keep evil away.
Many times have I fallen today, Mother dear.
Many graces neglected since last I knelt here.
Wilt you not in pity, my own Mother mild,
Ask Jesus to pardon the sins of your child?
I am going to rest for the day's work is done.
Its hours and its moments have passed one by
   one,
And the God who will judge me has counted
   them all.

He has numbered each grace, He has counted
    each fall.
In His book they are written against the last
    day —
O Mother, ask Jesus to wash the sins away,
For one drop of His blood, which for sinners
    was shed,
Is sufficient to cleanse the whole world from its
    guilt.
And if ere the dawn I should draw my last
    breath
And the sleep that I take be the long sleep of
    death,
Be near me, dear Mother, for Jesus' sake
When my soul on eternity's shore shall awake.

Night Prayer

Now I lay me down to sleep,
I pray the Lord my soul to keep.
Four corners to my bed,
Four angels there are spread:
Two to foot and two to head,
And four to carry me when I'm dead.
If any danger come to me,
Sweet Jesus Christ deliver me.
And if I die before I wake,
I pray the Lord my soul to take.

Short Version

Now I lay me down to sleep,
I pray the Lord my soul to keep.
If I should die before I wake,
I pray the Lord my soul to take.
God bless N.
God bless N.
Amen.

The *Nunc Dimittis*
(Canticle of Simeon)

(Luke 2:29-32)

Lord, now you let your servant go in peace;
your word has been fulfilled:

my own eyes have seen the salvation
which you have prepared in the sight of every
    people:

a light to reveal you to the nations
and the glory of your people Israel.[8]

*(The Church prays this canticle during night prayer
in the Liturgy of the Hours.)*

PRAYERS THROUGHOUT THE YEAR

ADVENT

The Church's liturgical year begins with the season of Advent. It begins on the Sunday closest to November 30 and ends with the Christmas Vigil Mass. In Advent, a time of joyful expectation, we focus on and prepare for the remembrance of Jesus' first coming in Bethlehem and His Second Coming at the end of time.

The Archangel's Greeting

Prayerfully meditate on these words spoken by Gabriel to the Blessed Virgin Mary:

"And behold, you will conceive in your womb and bear a son, and you shall call his name Jesus.
He will be great, and will be called the Son of
    the Most High;
and the Lord God will give to him the throne of
    his father David,
and he will reign over the house of Jacob for ever;
and of his kingdom there will be no end"
    (Lk 1:31-33).

The Messianic Prophecies

Advent is an ideal time to review the Messianic Prophecies. There are five significant stories in the Old Testament where the coming of the Messiah is foretold:

1. **Born of the House of David**
   Prophecy: 2 Samuel 7:12-16;
   Psalms 89:2-52, 132:11
   Fulfilled: Matthew 1:1-25

2. **Virgin Birth**
   Prophecy: Isaiah 7:14
   Fulfilled: Matthew 1:20-25

3. **Bethlehem**
   Prophecy: Micah 5:1-3
   Fulfilled: Matthew 2:5-6

4. **Wise Men and Their Gifts**
   Prophecy: Isaiah 49:23, 60:5 and
   Psalm 72:10-15
   Fulfilled: Matthew 2:9-12

5. **Holy Innocents**
   Prophecy: Jeremiah 31:15
   Fulfilled: Matthew 2:16-18

Prayer to St. Nicholas

God, our Father,
>we pray that through the intercession of St.
>>Nicholas
>you will protect our children.

Keep them safe from harm
>and help them grow and become worthy in
>>your sight.

Give them strength to keep their faith in you;
>and to keep alive their joy in your creation.

Through Jesus Christ, Our Lord.

Amen.

(The feast day of St. Nicholas is December 6.)

Advent Prayer

By Henri J. M. Nouwen (1932-1996)

Lord Jesus,

Master of both the light and the darkness,

send your Holy Spirit upon our preparations for
>Christmas.

We who have so much to do seek quiet spaces to
>hear your voice each day.

We who are anxious over many things look
>forward to your coming among us.

We who are blessed in so many ways long for
>the complete joy of your kingdom.

We whose hearts are heavy seek the joy of your
    presence.
We are your people, walking in darkness, yet
    seeking the light.
To you we say, "Come, Lord Jesus!"
Amen.

Prayer to Our Lady of Guadalupe

Our Lady of Guadalupe, mystical Rose, make intercession for our Holy Church, protect the Pope,
help all those who invoke you in their necessities, and since you are the ever-Virgin Mary and
Mother of the true God, obtain for us from your
most Holy Son the grace of keeping our faith,
sweet hope in the midst of the bitterness of life,
burning charity, and the precious gift of final perseverance.
    Amen.

*(Our Lady appeared to Juan Diego near Mexico City
in 1531 and left her image on his cloak. She is patron
of the Americas. Feast: December 12.)*

O Antiphons

*These antiphons are prayed each day at the Mag-
nificat of Evening Prayer from December 17 to
December 23. Authors unknown, these prayers are
from the ninth century or earlier.*

December 17:

O Wisdom, O holy Word of God,
you govern all creation with
your strong yet tender care.
Come and show your people the way to salvation.

December 18:

O sacred Lord of ancient Israel,
who showed yourself to Moses in the burning
    bush,
who gave him the holy law on Sinai mountain:
come, stretch out your mighty hand to set us free.

December 19:

O Flower of Jesse's stem,
you have been raised up as a sign for all peoples;
kings stand silent in your presence;
the nations bow down in worship before you.
Come, let nothing keep you from coming to
    our aid.

December 20:

O Key of David, O royal Power of Israel
controlling at your will the gate of heaven:
come, break down the prison walls of death
for those who dwell in darkness and the shadow
    of death;
and lead your captive people into freedom.

December 21:

O Radiant Dawn, splendor of eternal light, sun
      of justice:
come, shine on those who dwell in darkness
and the shadow of death.

December 22:

O King of all the nations,
the only joy of every human heart;
O Keystone of the mighty arch of man,
come and save the creature you fashioned from
      the dust.

December 23:

O Emmanuel, king and lawgiver,
desire of the nations,
Savior of all people,
come and set us free, Lord our God.[1]

——————— CHRISTMAS ———————

*At Christmas, December 25, we celebrate the coming
of Our Lord Jesus Christ, born of the Virgin Mary.
The Christmas season begins with the Vigil Mass
of Christmas and ends with the celebration of the
Baptism of the Lord.*

Christmas Prayer

By Gerard Manley Hopkins (1844-1889)

Moonless darkness stands between.
Past, the Past, no more be seen!
But the Bethlehem-star may lead me
To the sight of Him Who freed me
From the self that I have been.
Make me pure, Lord: Thou art holy;
Make me meek, Lord: Thou wert lowly;
Now beginning, and alway:
Now begin, on Christmas day.

Christmas Novena

Hail, and blessed be the hour and moment
At which the Son of God was born
Of a most pure Virgin
At a stable at midnight in Bethlehem
In the piercing cold
At that hour vouchsafe, I beseech Thee,
To hear my prayers and grant my desires
(mention your request here).
Through Jesus Christ and His most blessed
    Mother. Amen.

(Recite prayer for nine consecutive days.)

The Twelve Days of Christmas

Developed from an English hymn in 1645 called "In Those Twelve Days." Each number is a symbol for a truth of the faith and was often used as a teaching tool.

- ONE PARTRIDGE IN A PEAR TREE = The one true God
- TWO TURTLE DOVES = The two Testaments, Old and New
- THREE FRENCH HENS = The three Persons of the Trinity
- FOUR COLLEY (OR CALLING) BIRDS = The Four Evangelists
- FIVE GOLDEN RINGS = The five books of the Pentateuch (in the Bible)
- SIX GEESE A-LAYING = The six jars of water at Cana (Jesus' first miracle)
- SEVEN SWANS A-SWIMMING = The Seven Sacraments
- EIGHT MAIDS A-MILKING = The Eight Beatitudes
- NINE DRUMMERS DRUMMING = The nine choirs of angels
- TEN PIPERS PIPING = The Ten Commandments
- ELEVEN LADIES DANCING = The eleven faithful apostles (or the eleven stars seen in the Old Testament)
- TWELVE LORDS A-LEAPING = The Twelve Tribes of Israel (or the Twelve Apostles)[2]

Prayer for Christmas

Attributed to St. Bernard of Clairvaux

Let your goodness, Lord, appear to us, that we, made in your image, may conform ourselves to it. In our own strength we cannot image your majesty, power, and wonder; nor is it fitting for us to try. But your mercy reaches from the heavens, through the clouds, to the earth below. You have come to us as a small child, but you have brought us the greatest of all gifts, the gift of your eternal love. Caress us with your tiny hands, embrace us with your tiny arms, and pierce our hearts with your soft, sweet cries.[3]

Prayer for a Blessing on the New Year

O sacred and adorable Trinity,
hear our prayers on behalf of our Holy Father,
     the Pope,
our bishops, our clergy, and for all that are in
     authority over us.
Bless, we beseech You, during the coming year,
     the whole Catholic Church;
convert heretics and unbelievers;
soften the hearts of sinners so that they may
     return to Your friendship;
give prosperity to our country and peace among
     the nations of the world;
pour down Your blessings upon our friends,

relatives, and acquaintances, and upon our
enemies, if we have any;
assist the poor and the sick;
have pity on the souls of those whom this past
year has taken from us;
and be merciful to those who during the
coming year will be summoned before Your
judgment seat.
May all our actions be preceded by Your
inspirations and carried on by Your
assistance, so that all our prayers and works,
having been begun in You, may likewise be
ended through You. Amen.

Mary, Mother of God

By Pope St. John Paul II

Hail Mary, Mother of Christ and of the
Church!
Hail our life, our sweetness, and our hope!

To your care I entrust the necessities of all families,
the joys of children,
the desires of the young,
the worries of adults,
the pain of the sick,
the serene old age of senior citizens!

I entrust to you the fidelity of your Son's
ministers,

the hope of all those preparing themselves for
   this ministry,
the joyous dedication of virgins in cloisters,
the prayer and concern of men and women
   religious,
the lives and the commitment of all those who
   work for Christ's reign on earth.[4]

*(January 1 is the feast of Mary, the Holy Mother
of God.)*

Prayer for Peace

Merciful Father,
We are together on Earth, alone in the universe.
Look at us and help us to love one another.
Teach us to understand each other, just as you
   understand us.
Make our souls as fresh as the morning.
Make our hearts as innocent as the Lamb.
May we forgive each other, and forget the past,
and may we have peace inside — and in our
   world.
Today and forever. Amen.

The Epiphany

*By Bl. Columba Marmion, O.S.B. (1858-1923)
(Feast: October 3)*

O God, who, upon this day by the leading of
a star, did reveal Your only begotten Son to the

Gentiles; mercifully grant, that we, who already know You by faith, may be brought to the contemplation of the beauty of Your majesty.

Blessing of the Home and Household on Epiphany

The traditional date of Epiphany is January 6, but in the United States it is celebrated on the Sunday between January 2 and 8. In many homes, it is customary to mark the initials KMB for Kaspar, Melchior, and Balthasar, with crosses between them and the year on either side of the initials at the top of entrance doors with blessed chalk.

God of Bethlehem and Cana,
　　God of Jordan's leaping waters,
in baptism you bring us
　　into your family.

You wed us and embrace us
　　as your beloved.
May we fill this place
　　with kindness to one another,
　　with hospitality to guests,
　　and with abundant care
　　　　for every stranger.

By the gentle light of a star,
　　guide home all who seek you
　　on paths of faith, hope, and love.

Then we will join the angels in proclaiming
   your praise:
Glory in heaven and peace on earth,
   now and forever. Amen.[5]

LENT

*Lent, the penitential season before Easter, begins with
Ash Wednesday. During this season, we are called
to prayer, fasting, and almsgiving. We should also
perform works of charity, penance, and other devotional practices (such as the Stations of the Cross).*

ASH WEDNESDAY
Blessing of the Season and
of a Place of Prayer

*Traditionally, people set aside a place for prayer
during the Lenten season. The Bible, a crucifix, and
a candle are put there. The candle is lighted during
prayer times.*

All make the sign of the cross as the leader begins:

The Lord calls us to days of penance and mercy.
Blessed be the name of the Lord.
All respond: Now and forever.

*The leader may use these or similar words to intro-
duce the blessing:*

Remember that we are but dust and ashes, yet by God's grace we have died in Baptism and have put on the Lord Jesus Christ. Each year we keep these Forty Days with prayer and penance and the practice of charity so that we may come to the Easter festival ready to renew once more the life-giving commitment of our Baptism. Through this Lent we shall gather here to read the Scriptures and ponder them and to intercede with God for our needs and for the needs of the Church and the world.

Then the Scripture is read:

Listen to the words of the Prophet Isaiah: *(Read Isaiah 58:5-10 [or Deuteronomy 30:15-20].)*

The reader concludes: The Word of the Lord.
All respond: Thanks be to God.

After a time of silence, members of the household offer prayers of intercession for the world, the Church and its catechumens, and themselves. The leader then invites:

Let us kneel and ask God's blessing on us and on this holy season.

After a short silence, the leader continues:

Merciful God,
you called us forth from the dust of the earth;
you claimed us for Christ in the waters of
   Baptism.
Look upon us as we enter these Forty Days
bearing the mark of ashes,
and bless our journey through the desert of Lent
to the font of rebirth.
May our fasting be hunger for justice;
our alms, a making of peace;
our prayer, the chant of humble and grateful
   hearts.

All that we do and pray is in the name of Jesus,
for in his Cross you proclaim your love
forever and ever.

All respond: Amen.

*Each person then kisses the crucifix. All then stand,
and the leader concludes:*

All through these days let us be quiet and prayerful, pondering the mysteries told in the Scriptures.
In the Cross, we have been claimed for Christ. In
Christ, we make the prayer that fills these days
of mercy:

Our Father ...

The leader says: Let us bless the Lord.
All respond: Thanks be to God.

(The blessing may conclude with a song such as "Praise God from Whom All Blessings Flow" or "The Glory of These Forty Days.")[6]

Prayer to Be Generous

Thank you, dear God, for all the things that you have given me: family, food, clothing, and home. You have given me health, a mind, and free will. Best of all, dear God, you have given me the gift of true faith. Help me to share with others the love you give to me.

Amen.[7]

MORE PRAYERS FOR LENT

Prayer When Seeing or Remembering the Catechumens

Lord, look with love on the catechumens through this time of preparation.

Enfold them within your Church.

At Table During Weekdays of Lent

Begin after a short silence. The leader alternates with the others who are present.

V. I was hungry.
R. And you gave me food.

V. I was thirsty.
R. And you gave me drink.

V. I was a stranger.
R. And you welcomed me.

V. I was naked.
R. And you clothed me.

V. I was ill.
R. And you comforted me.

V. I was in jail.
R. And you came to see me.

The leader prays:
Lord Jesus Christ,
may our Lenten fasting turn us
    toward all our brothers and sisters who are
    in need.
Bless this table, our good food, and ourselves.
Send us through Lent with good cheer,
and bring us to the fullness of your passover.
R. Amen.[8]

Stations of the Cross (Way of the Cross)

The Stations ideally are prayed in a church, moving from one Station to the next. Stations may be prayed with a group or by individuals. If done individually, it is best to pray silently so as not to disturb others in the church. There are many versions of the Stations. The following is one example:

After an introductory prayer, each station usually begins with:

V. We adore you, O Christ, and we praise you.
R. Because by your holy Cross you have re-deemed the world.

At each station, a meditation is made and a prayer may be added. Suggested Scripture texts appear after the stations. In public devotions, a verse of the Stabat Mater *(see page 38) is often sung after each station.*

- *The First Station:* Jesus is condemned to death. (Mt 27:26; Mk 15:15; Lk 23:23-25; Jn 19:16)

- *The Second Station:* Jesus is made to carry the cross. (Jn 19:17)

- *The Third Station:* Jesus falls the first time. (Mt 27:31)

- *The Fourth Station:* Jesus meets his Blessed Mother. (Jn 19:25-27)

- *The Fifth Station:* Simon helps Jesus carry his cross. (Mt 27:32; Mk 15:21; Lk 23:26)

- *The Sixth Station:* Veronica wipes the face of Jesus. (Lk 23:27)

- *The Seventh Station:* Jesus falls the second time. (Lk 23:26)

- *The Eighth Station:* Jesus speaks to the women of Jerusalem. (Lk 23:28-31)

- *The Ninth Station:* Jesus falls the third time. (Jn 19:17)

- *The Tenth Station:* Jesus is stripped of his garments. (Lk 23:34)

- *The Eleventh Station:* Jesus is nailed to the cross. (Mt 27:33-38; Mk 15:22-27; Lk 23:33-34; Jn 19:18)

- *The Twelfth Station:* Jesus dies on the cross. (Mt 27:46-50; Mk 15:34-37; Lk 23:46; Jn 19:28-30)

- *The Thirteenth Station:* Jesus is taken down from the cross. (Mk 27:57-58; Mk 15:42-45; Lk 28:50-52; Jn 19:38)

- *The Fourteenth Station:* Jesus is placed in the tomb. (Mt 27:59-61; Mk 15:46-47; Lk 23:53-56; Jn 19:39-42)

- *The Fifteenth Station* (optional): The Resurrection. (Mt 28; Mk 16; Lk 24; Jn 20)

The Stations are usually concluded with prayers for the intentions of the Holy Father: for example, an Our Father, a Hail Mary, and a Glory Be.

(The Stations of the Cross is an ancient devotion brought back from the Holy Land, where pilgrims retraced the footsteps of Jesus on the road to Calvary.)

A Prayer for Passion Sunday

By St. Clare of Assisi

Praise and glory to you, O loving Jesus Christ,
for the most sacred wound in your side ...
   and for your infinite mercy
which you have made known to us in the opening
   of your breast to the soldier Longinus,
and so to us all.

I pray you, O most gentle Jesus,
having redeemed me by baptism
   from original sin,
so now, by your Precious Blood,
   which is offered and received
   throughout the world,
deliver me from all evils,
past, present and to come.

And, by your most bitter death,
give me a lively faith,
   a firm hope, and
   a perfect charity,

so that I may love you
   with all my heart
   and all my soul,
   and all my strength;
make me firm and steadfast
   in good works
and grant me perseverance
   in your service
so that I may be able to please you always.
Amen.

———————— EASTER TRIDUUM ————————

*The Triduum begins Holy Thursday at the evening
Mass with the celebration of the Lord's Supper and
ends with Evening Prayer on Easter. Good Friday
is a day of fast and abstinence. Some continue the
fast until the Easter Vigil on Holy Saturday. Fasting
from food, work, and entertainment should be observed in anticipation of the Church's greatest feast of
the liturgical year – Easter. These days in particular
should be kept holy.*

At Table During the Easter Triduum

For our sake Christ was obedient,
accepting even death, death on a cross.
Therefore God raised him on high
and gave him the name above all other names.[9]

HOLY THURSDAY EVENING

Holy Thursday signals the end of Lent. After evening Mass, time should be spent in prayer. Prayers before the Blessed Sacrament in honor of Jesus celebrating the Last Supper and instituting the sacrament of Eucharist are appropriate, as well as meditation on Scripture (Matthew 26:17-30; Mark 14:12-25; Luke 22:1-38; John, chapters 13-17, Psalm 22, and Lamentations).

Jesus Gives Us the Holy Eucharist

(1 Corinthians 11:23-26)

For I received from the Lord what I also delivered to you, that the Lord Jesus on the night when he was betrayed took bread, and when he had given thanks, he broke it, and said, "This is my body which is for you. Do this in remembrance of me." In the same way also the cup, after supper, saying, "This cup is the new covenant in my blood. Do this, as often as you drink it, in remembrance of me." For as often as you eat this bread and drink the cup, you proclaim the Lord's death until he comes.

GOOD FRIDAY

Veneration of the Holy Cross and reading of the Passion of Our Lord (Jn 18:1-19:42; cf. Mt 26:31-61; Mk 14:26-15:39; Lk 22:39-23:49; Jn 18-19) is observed, particularly between noon and 3 p.m.

The Seven Last Words of Jesus Upon the Cross

- *First Word:* "Father, forgive them; for they know not what they do." (Lk 23:34)
- *Second Word:* "I say to you, today you will be with me in Paradise." (Lk 23:43)
- *Third Word:* "Behold, your son … behold, your mother." (Jn 19:26-27)
- *Fourth Word:* "My God, my God, why have you forsaken me?" (Mt 27:46; Mk15:34, RSV-SCE)
- *Fifth Word:* "I thirst." (Jn 19:28)
- *Sixth Word:* "It is finished." (Jn 19:30)
- *Seventh Word:* "Father, into your hands I commit my spirit!" (Lk 23:46, RSV-SCE)

"Glory Be to Jesus"

1. Glory be to Jesus,
Who, in bitter pains,
Poured for me the life-blood
From His sacred veins.

2. Grace and life eternal
In that blood I find;
Blest be His compassion,
Infinitely kind!

3. Blest through endless ages
Be the precious stream,
Which from endless torments
Did the world redeem.

4. Abel's blood for vengeance
Pleaded to the skies;
But the blood of Jesus
For our pardon cries.

5. Oft as it is sprinkled
On our guilty hearts,
Satan in confusion
Terror-struck departs.

6. Oft as earth exulting
Wafts its praise on high,
Angel-hosts rejoicing
Make their glad reply.

7. Lift ye then your voices;
Swell the mighty flood;
Louder still and louder
Praise the precious blood.[10]

Holy Saturday

Fast and waiting continue. Prayers on behalf of those entering the Church during the Easter Vigil are recommended.

Lord,
> we pray to you for the elect,
> who have now accepted for themselves
> the loving purpose and the mysteries
> that you revealed in the life of your Son.
May they have faith in their hearts
> and accomplish your will in their lives.

We ask this through Christ our Lord.
R. Amen.

Easter Vigil

Baptismal Promises and the Creed (Apostles' Creed, page 15, or Nicene Creed, page 153) are said. The Easter Triduum closes with Evening Prayer on Easter Sunday.

Baptismal Promises

V. Do you reject Satan?
R. I do.
V. And all his work?
R. I do.
V. And all his empty promises?
R. I do.

V. Do you believe in God, the Father Almighty, creator of heaven and earth?

R. I do.

V. Do you believe in Jesus Christ, his only Son, our Lord, who was born of the Virgin Mary, was crucified, died, and was buried, rose from the dead, and is now seated at the right hand of the Father?

R. I do.

V. Do you believe in the Holy Spirit, the holy catholic Church, the communion of saints, the forgiveness of sins, the resurrection of the body, and life everlasting?

R. I do.

The priest concludes:

V. God, the all-powerful Father of our Lord Jesus Christ, has given us a new birth by water and the Holy Spirit, and forgiven all our sins.

May he also keep us faithful to our Lord Jesus Christ for ever and ever.

R. Amen.[11]

EASTER

Easter is the culmination of the Church Year, the Sunday of Sundays, the Feast of feasts. The theme of Easter is resurrection from sin and death to the life of grace. Easter Sunday begins the Easter Season, which lasts fifty days.

A Prayer at Easter
Attributed to St. Bernard of Clairvaux

Lord, you have passed over into new life, and you now invite us to pass over also. In these past days we have grieved at your suffering and mourned at your death. We have given ourselves over to repentance and prayer, to abstinence and gravity. Now at Easter you tell us that we have died to sin. Yet, if this be true, how can we remain on earth? How can we pass over to your risen life, while we are still in this world? Will we not be just as meddlesome, just as lazy, just as selfish as before? Will we not still be bad-tempered and stubborn, enmeshed in all the vices of the past? We pray that as we pass over to you, our faces will never look back. Instead, let us, like you, make heaven on earth.

Resurrection Prayer

Heavenly Father, Lord of life and death,
when Christ our Paschal Lamb was sacrificed,
he overcame death by his own dying
and restored us to life by his own rising.
In virtue of his life-giving Passover,
pour your Holy Spirit into our hearts,
fill us with awe and reverence for you,
and with love and compassion for our neighbor.
We ask this through the same Christ our Lord.
All: Amen.[12]

Blessing of Easter Foods

*After the Lenten fast, the foods of the Easter feast
are particularly sweet. In many places, the food for
Easter dinner is brought to the church to be blessed
on Holy Saturday.*

God of glory,
the eyes of all turn to you
as we celebrate Christ's victory over sin and
  death.

Bless us and this food of our first Easter meal.
May we who gather at the Lord's table,
continue to celebrate the joy of his Resurrection
and be admitted finally to his heavenly banquet.

Grant this through Christ our Lord.
R. Amen.[13]

Blessing of Easter Eggs

We beseech Thee, O Lord, to bestow Thy benign blessing upon these eggs, to make them a wholesome food for Thy faithful, who gratefully partake of them in honor of the Resurrection of Our Lord Jesus Christ.

— PENTECOST —

The fiftieth day after Easter, the feast of Pentecost concludes the Easter Season. Many refer to it as the "birthday" of the Church. It reminds us of the Holy Spirit coming to the apostles as they were gathered in the upper room.

Veni, Sancte Spiritus

(See page 31.)

Come, Holy Spirit, Creator Blest
(*Veni, Creator Spiritus*)

(See page 33.)

Prayer by St. Alphonsus Liguori for the Seven Gifts of the Holy Spirit

Holy Spirit, divine Consoler,
I adore you as my true God,
   with God the Father and God the Son.
I adore you and unite myself to the adoration
   you receive from the angels and saints.

I give you my heart and I offer my ardent
    thanksgiving
for all the grace which you never cease to bestow
    on me.

O Giver of all supernatural gifts who filled the
    soul of the Blessed Virgin Mary, Mother of
    God, with such immense favors, I beg you
    to visit me with your grace and your love
    and to grant me the *gift of holy fear*, so that it
    may act on me as a check to prevent me from
    falling back into my past sins, for which I beg
    pardon.

Grant me the *gift of piety*,
    so that I may serve you
    for the future with increased fervor,
    follow with more promptness your holy
        inspirations,
    and observe your divine precepts with greater
        fidelity.

Give me the *gift of knowledge*,
    so that I may know the things of God,
    and enlightened by your holy teaching,
    may walk, without deviation,
    in the path of eternal salvation.

Give me the *gift of fortitude*,
    so that I may overcome courageously
    all the assaults of the devil,
    and all the dangers of this world
    which threaten the salvation of my soul.

Give me the *gift of counsel*,
    so that I may choose what is more conducive
    to my spiritual advancement,
    and may discover the wiles and snares of the
        tempter.

Give me the *gift of understanding*,
    so that I may apprehend the divine mysteries,
    and by contemplation of heavenly things
    detach my thoughts and affections
    from the vain things of this passing world.

Give me the *gift of wisdom*,
    so that I may rightly direct all my actions,
    referring them to God as my last end;
    so that, having loved and served him in this
        life,
    I may have the happiness of possessing him
        eternally in the next.
Amen.

Prayer for Pentecost

O God, who on this day taught the hearts of your faithful people by sending to them the light of your Holy Spirit: Grant us by the same Spirit to have a right judgment in all things, and evermore to rejoice in his holy comfort; through Jesus Christ your Son our Lord, who lives and reigns with you, in the unity of the Holy Spirit, one God, for ever and ever. Amen.[14]

─── FEAST DAYS AND ─── DAYS OF CELEBRATION

St. Elizabeth Ann Seton

(January 4)

Lord God,
you blessed Elizabeth Seton with gifts of
    grace
as wife and mother, educator and foundress,
so that she might spend her life in service to
    your people.
Through her example and prayers
may we learn to express our love for you
in love for our fellow men and women.
We ask this through our Lord Jesus Christ, your
    Son,

who lives and reigns with you and the Holy
    Spirit,
one God, for ever and ever. Amen.[15]

*(St. Elizabeth Ann Bayley Seton, 1774-1821, was
the first American-born saint to be canonized. She
was a convert to Catholicism and founded the Sisters
of Charity in the U.S.)*

St. John Neumann

(January 5)

Father,
you called John Neumann to labor for the
    gospel
among the people of the new world.
His ministry strengthened many others in the
    Christian faith:
through his prayers may faith grow strong in
    this land.
Grant this through our Lord Jesus Christ, your
    Son,
who lives and reigns with you and the Holy
    Spirit,
one God for ever and ever. Amen.[16]

*(St. John Neumann, 1811-1860, bishop of Philadel-
phia, helped spread Forty Hours Devotion. He was
the first U.S. bishop to be canonized a saint.)*

St. André Bessette

(January 6)

Blessed Brother André, your devotion to St. Joseph
is an inspiration to us. You gave your life selflessly
to bring the message of his life to others. Pray that
we may learn from St. Joseph, and from you, what
it is like to care for Jesus and do his work in the
world. Amen.

*(St. André Bessette, 1845-1937, was a Canadian
Holy Cross brother who was instrumental in building
St. Joseph's Oratory in Montreal, Canada.)*

Prayer for Christian Unity

(January 18-25)

Almighty and eternal God,
you gather the scattered sheep
and watch over those you have gathered.
Look kindly on all who follow Jesus, your Son.
You have marked them with the seal of one
    baptism,
now make them one in the fullness of faith
and unite them in the bond of love.
We ask this through Christ our Lord.
R. Amen.[17]

Candlemas or Presentation of Our Lord

(February 2)

Candles are blessed on this feast that is celebrated forty days after Christmas. Commemorating the presentation of the baby Jesus in the Temple, we recall the prophecy of Simeon that Jesus Christ would be "a light for revelation to the Gentiles, and for glory to your people Israel" (Lk 2:32, RSV-SCE). The feast was formerly called the Presentation of Mary.

Our Lady of Lourdes

(February 11)

Our Lady of Lourdes, please come to the assistance of all those who are suffering. Amen.

(From February 11 through July 16, 1858, the Blessed Virgin Mary appeared 18 times to St. Bernadette Soubirous at Lourdes. Mary identified herself as the Immaculate Conception. A spring of healing waters appeared at the grotto where the apparitions occurred, drawing millions of pilgrims each year. The feast has become a day of prayer for the sick and suffering and those who care for them.)

St. Katharine Drexel

(March 3)

Ever-loving God, you called St. Katharine Drexel to teach the message of the Gospel and to bring the life of the Eucharist to the African American and Native American peoples. By her prayers and example, enable us to work for justice among the poor and oppressed, and keep us undivided in love in the eucharistic community of your Church. We ask this through Christ our Lord.

Amen.

(St. Katharine Drexel, 1858-1955, Philadelphia-born heiress, founded the Sisters of the Blessed Sacrament for Indians and Colored People.)

St. Patrick

(March 17)

St. Patrick's Breastplate

I arise today through

God's strength to pilot me,
God's might to uphold me,
God's wisdom to guide me,
God's eye to see before me,
God's ear to hear me,
God's word to speak for me,
God's hand to guard me,
God's way to lie before me,

God's shield to protect me,
God's host to secure me —
   against snares of the devil,
   against temptations and vices,
   against inclinations of nature,
   against everyone who shall wish me ill, afar
     and near,
   alone and in a crowd....

Christ be with me, Christ before me,
   Christ behind me,
Christ in me, Christ beneath me,
   Christ above me,
Christ be on my right, Christ be on my left,
Christ where I lie, Christ where I sit,
   Christ where I arise,
Christ in the heart of everyone who thinks
   of me,
Christ in the mouth of everyone who speaks
   of me,
Christ in every eye that sees me,
Christ in every ear that hears me.

Salvation is of the Lord.
Salvation is of the Lord.
Salvation is of Christ.
May your salvation, O Lord, be ever with us.

(St. Patrick, 389-461, is known for his missionary work and the conversion of Ireland.)

St. Joseph
(March 19)

Grant, we pray, almighty God,
that by Saint Joseph's intercession
your Church may constantly watch over
the unfolding of the mysteries of human
    salvation,
whose beginnings you entrusted to his faithful
    care.
Through our Lord Jesus Christ, your Son,
who lives and reigns with you
    in the unity of the Holy Spirit,
one God, for ever and ever. Amen.[18]

Prayer to St. Joseph

O Glorious St. Joseph, chosen by God to be the
foster father of Jesus, the chaste spouse of Mary
ever-Virgin, and head of the Holy Family, be
the heavenly patron and defender of the Church
founded by Jesus.

With confidence we beg your powerful aid for
the Church on earth. Shield it with paternal love,
especially the Supreme Pontiff, together with all
the bishops and priests who are in union with
the Holy See. Be the defender of all who labor
for souls.

Protect the working men and women and
their families. Intercede for young people who

are searching for their place in life. Be the sure
refuge for all of us at the hour of death, and guide
us safely into heaven.

In Jesus' name we pray.

Amen.

*(March 19 is a time of feasting that is shared with
all, especially the poor, in celebration of St. Joseph,
spouse of Mary our Blessed Mother and foster father
of Jesus.)*

Mother's Day

(Second Sunday in May)

(This prayer may be used at the dinner table.)

Loving God,

as a mother gives life and nourishment to her
        children,

so you watch over your Church.

Bless our mother.

Let the example of her faith and love shine
        forth.

Grant that we, her family,

may honor her always

with a spirit of profound respect.

Grant this through Christ our Lord.

R. Amen.[19]

Memorial Day
(Last Monday in May)

Memorial Day

By Joyce Kilmer

The bugle echoes shrill and sweet,
But not of war it sings today.
The road is rhythmic with the feet
Of men-at-arms who come to pray.

The rose blossoms white and red
On tombs where weary soldiers lie;
Flags wave above the honored dead
And martial music cleaves the sky.

Above their wreath-strewn graves we kneel,
They kept the faith and fought the fight.
Through flying lead and crimson steel
They plunged for Freedom and the Right.

May we, their grateful children, learn
Their strength, who lie beneath this sod,
Who went through fire and death to earn
At last the accolade of God.

In shining rank on rank arrayed,
They march, the legions of the Lord;
He is their Captain unafraid,
The Prince of Peace … Who brought a sword.

Prayer of a Soldier
By Joyce Kilmer (1918)

My shoulders ache beneath my pack
(Lie easier, Cross, upon His back).

I march with feet that burn and smart
(Tread, Holy Feet, upon my heart).

Men shout at me who may not speak
(They scourged Your back and smote Your
    cheek).

I may not lift a hand to clear
My eyes of salty drops that sear.

(Then shall my fickle soul forget
Your Agony of Bloody Sweat?)

My rifle hand is still and numb
(From Your pierced palm red rivers come).

Lord, Thou did suffer more for me
Than all the hosts of land and sea.

So let me render back again
This millionth of Your gift. Amen.

*(Joyce Kilmer, 1886-1918, American writer, poet,
and convert to Catholicism, was killed in action in
France during World War I.)*

Father's Day

(Third Sunday in June)

God our Father,
in your wisdom and love you made all things.
Bless our father.
Let the example of his faith and love shine
    forth.
Grant that we, his family,
may honor him always
with a spirit of profound respect.
Grant this through Christ our Lord.
R. Amen.[20]

A Father's Prayer

St. Joseph,
head of the Holy Family,
grant me the spiritual gifts and virtues I need
to fulfill my duties as head of the family
    entrusted to me by God.

With the help of my wife,
may I discharge the God-given responsibilities
    with devotion and respect,
with faith and charity.
Following your example,
may I bring to my daily task the care and respect
that will really make it a collaboration to God's
    work
and a true service to men, my brothers.

In spite of social conditions and spells of
    sickness,
may I earn enough to supply my family with
    food and lodging,
clothing and education,
in the joy of a hearth safe from distress.

Teach me the true virtues of a husband and
    Christian educator.
As you went to great pains to feed and educate
    Jesus,
the child of God entrusted to your care,
grant that I may bring up my children with love
    and firmness,
with intelligence and tact;
that I may pray with them and explain to them,
when and how I must,
their obligations as Christians,
by word and act;
may I stay calm and patient when they fail
    and err,
without fear of admonishing and correcting
    them when I must.
May I give to each one,
according to his or her character and
    personality,
the necessary incentives,
with special attention and affection.
May I not be too often absent from home,
since my wife and children require my presence.

O St. Joseph,
grant that I may always live as a true Christian,
and observe the fidelity,
the love, and devotion I owe to my wife and
    children,
since I have received from God the difficult and
    wonderful mission of leading them all to
    His Kingdom. Amen.[21]

Prayer to the Apostles Ss. Peter and Paul

(June 29)

O holy Apostles Peter and Paul, intercede for us.
Protect, O Lord, your people who trust in the
patronage of your Apostles, Peter and Paul, and
by their constant protection protect your people.
Through Christ our Lord.
    Amen.[22]

*(Jesus made the fisherman Peter the chief of the apos-
tles and head of the Church, the first pope. St. Peter
was martyred by crucifixion in 64 or 65. After perse-
cuting Christians, St. Paul experienced a conversion
on the road to Damascus and became the Apostle to
the Gentiles through extensive missionary journeys
before being martyred in 64 or 67.)*

St. Junípero Serra

(July 1)

God most high,
your servant Junípero Serra
brought the gospel of Christ
to the peoples of Mexico and California
and firmly established the Church among them.
By his intercession,
and through the example of his evangelical zeal,
inspire us to be faithful witnesses of Jesus
    Christ,
who lives and reigns with you and the Holy
    Spirit,
one God, for ever and ever.
Amen.[23]

(St. Junípero Serra, 1713-1784, a Spanish Franciscan priest, founded nine of twenty-one missions in California. Feast: July 1.)

Independence Day

(July 4)

A Prayer for Religious Liberty

Almighty God, Father of all nations,
    For freedom you have set us free in Christ
    Jesus (Gal 5:1).
We praise and bless you for the gift of religious
    liberty,

the foundation of human rights, justice, and the
common good.
Grant to our leaders the wisdom to protect and
promote our liberties;
By your grace may we have the courage to
defend them, for ourselves and for all those
who live in this blessed land.
We ask this through the intercession of Mary
Immaculate, our patroness,
and in the name of your Son, our Lord Jesus
Christ, in the unity of the Holy Spirit,
with whom you live and reign, one God, for
ever and ever. Amen.[24]

Prayer for America
By Bishop John Carroll

We pray to Thee, O God of might, wisdom and
justice, through whom authority is rightly admin-
istered, laws are enacted, and judgments decreed,
assist with Your Holy Spirit of counsel and fortitude the President of the United States, that his
administration may be conducted in righteousness, and be eminently useful to Your people over
whom he presides, by encouraging due respect for
virtue and religion, by a faithful execution of the
laws in justice and mercy, and by restraining vice
and immorality.

Let the light of Your divine wisdom direct
the deliberations of Congress and shine forth in

all the proceedings and laws framed for our rule and government, so that they may tend to the preservation of peace, the promotion of national happiness, the increase of industry, sobriety, and useful knowledge; and may perpetuate to us the blessings of equal liberty.

(In 1789, Father John Carroll was named the first American bishop to the Diocese of Baltimore, which then encompassed the entire United States.)

St. Kateri Tekakwitha

(July 14)
O God, who desired the Virgin
[St.] Kateri Tekakwitha
to flower among Native Americans
in a life of innocence,
grant, through her intercession,
that when all are gathered into your Church
from every nation, tribe, and tongue,
they may magnify you
in a single canticle of praise.
Through our Lord Jesus Christ, your Son,
who lives and reigns with you in the unity of
the Holy Spirit,
one God, for ever and ever.[25]

(The mystic "Lily of the Mohawks," St. Kateri Tekak-witha, 1656-1690, was the first Native American named a saint.)

Assumption

(August 15)

A holy day of obligation, this day commemorates God taking Mary into heaven, body and soul, at the end of her earthly life. A long-held belief, this truth was proclaimed a dogma by Pope Pius XII on November 1, 1950.

O Jesus, you paid our debts by your death.
O dear Mother, you gave him to us so we could
    be saved.
God did not choose great people for his
    messengers and his channels of love.
Only the humble can see clearly.
And only they say we are nothing, and God is
    everything.
How blessed you are, dear Jesus, and how loving
    is your Mother.
Please help us and bless us.
Amen.

The world proclaims the gospel of money;
Jesus proclaims the gospel of love.
Help us, Mother, to love your Son more
and follow his holy Gospel. Amen.[26]

On the Assumption of Mary

By St. Alphonsus Liguori

O most sweet Lady and our Mother,
thou hast already left the earth and reached the
    kingdom,
where, as Queen, thou art enthroned above all
    the choirs of angels, as the Church sings;
    "She is exulted above the choirs of angels in
    the celestial kingdom."
We well know that we sinners are not worthy to
    possess thee in this valley of darkness;
    but we also know that thou, in thy greatness,
    hast never lost compassion for us poor
    children of Adam;
    nay, even that it is increased in thee.
From the high throne, then,
    to which thou art exalted,
    turn, O Mary,
    thy compassionate eyes upon us,
    and pity us.
Remember, also, that in leaving this world
    thou did promise not to forget us.
Look at us and succor us.
See in the midst of what tempests
    and danger we constantly are,
    and shall be until the end of our lives.
By the merits of thy happy death
    obtain us holy perseverance in the Divine
    friendship,

that we may finally quit this life in God's
grace;
and thus we also shall one day come to kiss thy
feet in Paradise,
and unite with the blessed spirits in praising thee
and singing thy glories as thou deserves. Amen.

Labor Day

(First Monday in September)

Prayer to St. Joseph for Workers
By Pope Pius XII

O glorious Patriarch St. Joseph, humble and just
craftsman of Nazareth, who gave, to all Christians
but particularly to us, an example of a perfect life
of diligent work in admirable unity with Mary and
Jesus! Help us in our daily work so that we also
may find there an effective means of glorifying our
Lord, of sanctifying ourselves and of being useful
to the society in which we live.

Obtain for us from our Lord, O beloved
protector, humility and simplicity of heart, at-
tachment to work, benevolence toward those who
work with us, compliance with the Divine Will
in the difficulties of this life and joy in bearing
them, awareness of our special mission and sense
of our social responsibility, a spirit of discipline
and prayer, humility and respect for our super-

visors, fraternity towards our co-workers, and charity toward those dependent on us.

Be with us in prosperity when everything invites us to enjoy the fruits of our labor, but be our support also in times of stress when the skies seem to close in upon us when even the tools of our work seem to rebel in our hands.

Grant that, following your example, we may hold fast to Mary, our Mother, your gentle spouse who was content to work quietly with you, that we may never turn our eyes from Jesus, who toiled with you at your carpenter's bench, so that we may lead a peaceful and holy life on earth, the prelude to that eternally happy one which awaits us in heaven forever more.

Amen.[27]

(Pope Pius XII, 1876-1958, was declared Venerable by Pope Benedict XVI in 2009.)

St. Mother Théodore Guérin

(October 3)

Jesus, only source of truth and life, who taught the world the way of salvation, grant us the grace which we humbly ask through your faithful servant Mother Théodore Guérin, who spent all her life to make you known and loved. May this grace be consolation for soul and body, and may it unite us ever more to you and to one another in life and in eternity. Amen.[28]

(St. Mother Théodore Guérin, 1798-1856, foundress of the Sisters of Providence of Saint Mary-of-the-Woods in Indiana, established schools and orphanages. Patron of the Diocese of Lafayette in Indiana.)

St. Francis

(October 4)

Lord, Make Me an Instrument of Your Peace

Inspired by St. Francis of Assisi

Lord, make me an instrument of Your peace:
Where there is hatred, let me sow love.
Where there is injury, pardon,
Where there is doubt, faith,
Where there is despair, hope,
Where there is darkness, light,
and where there is sadness, joy.

O Divine Master, grant that I may not so much
    seek to be consoled, as to console;
To be understood, as to understand;
To be loved, as to love;
For it is in giving that we receive,
It is in pardoning that we are pardoned
And it is in dying that we are born to eternal
    life.

Our Lady of the Rosary

(October 7)

If you are not accustomed to praying the Rosary, this would be an ideal day to try it. See pages 40-44 to learn how to pray this beautiful prayer.

St. Ignatius of Antioch

(October 17)

Letter to the Ephesians

Make an effort, then, to meet more frequently to celebrate God's Eucharist and to offer praise. For, when you meet frequently in the same place, the forces of Satan are overthrown, and his baneful influence is neutralized by the unanimity of your faith. Peace is a precious thing: it puts an end to every war waged by heavenly or earthly enemies.

Letter to the Romans

I am writing to all the Churches and I enjoin all, that I am dying willingly for God's sake, if only you do not prevent it. I beg you, do not do me an untimely kindness. Allow me to be eaten by the beasts, which are my way of reaching to God. I am God's wheat, and I am to be ground by the teeth of wild beasts, so that I may become the pure bread of Christ.

Letter to the Philadelphians

Take care, then, to partake of one Eucharist; for, one is the flesh of Our Lord Jesus Christ, and one the cup to unite us with His Blood, and one altar, just as there is one bishop assisted by the presbytery and the deacons, my fellow servants. Thus you will conform in all your actions to the will of God.

(St. Ignatius of Antioch, who died around the year 110, was the third bishop of Antioch. A disciple of the apostle John, St. Ignatius is known through his writings, particularly the epistles he wrote to various Christian communities while on his way from Antioch to his martyrdom in Rome.)

All Saints' Day

(November 1)

For All the Saints

By William W. How (1823-1897)

1. For all the saints who from their labors rest,
Who Thee by faith before the world confessed,
Thy name, O Jesus, be forever blest,
Alleluia! Alleluia!

2. Thou wast their Rock, their Fortress, and
   their Might;
Thou, Lord, their Captain in the well-fought fight;
Thou, in the darkness drear, their one true Light.
Alleluia! Alleluia!

3. Oh, may Thy soldiers, faithful, true and bold,
Fight as the saints who nobly fought of old
And win with them the victor's crown of gold.
Alleluia! Alleluia!

4. O blest communion, fellowship divine,
We feebly struggle, they in glory shine;
Yet all are one in Thee, for all are Thine.
Alleluia! Alleluia!

5. And when the fight is fierce, the warfare long,
Steals on the ear the distant triumph song,
And hearts are brave again, and arms are strong.
Alleluia! Alleluia!

6. But, lo, there breaks a yet more glorious day;
The saints triumphant rise in bright array;
The King of Glory passes on His way.
Alleluia! Alleluia!

7. From earth's wide bounds, from ocean's
farthest coast,
Through gates of pearl streams in the countless
host,
Singing to Father, Son, and Holy Ghost,
Alleluia! Alleluia!

8. The golden evening brightens in the west;
Soon, soon, to faithful warriors cometh rest.
Sweet is the calm of Paradise the blest.
Alleluia! Alleluia!

All Souls' Day
(November 2)

On this day, we pray especially for the Holy Souls in purgatory. It is a traditional time to visit the graves of loved ones. Another time to visit graves is on the anniversary of the date of their deaths.

Eternal Father, I offer You the most precious Blood of Your Divine Son, Jesus, in union with all the Masses said throughout the world today, for all the Holy Souls in Purgatory, for sinners everywhere, for sinners in the Universal Church, those in my own home and within my family. Amen.

(Dictated by Our Lord to St. Gertrude the Great.)

Visiting a Grave

The entire month of November is dedicated to remembering our deceased family members, saints and all those who have gone on to their eternal reward. On November 1, we particularly remember the saints. Many pray the Litany of the Saints (see page 103) on that day.

All make the Sign of the Cross. The leader begins:

Praise be to God our Father, who raised Jesus Christ from the dead. Blessed be God for ever.

All respond:
Blessed be God for ever.

One or more of the following Scripture passages may be read: 2 Corinthians 5:1 or Romans 8:38-39.

After a time of silence, all join in prayers of intercession or litanies. Then all join hands for the Lord's Prayer. The leader then prays:

Lord God,
whose days are without end
and whose mercies beyond counting,
keep us mindful
that life is short and the hour of death
    unknown.
Let your Spirit guide our days on earth
in the ways of holiness and justice,
that we may serve you
in union with the whole Church,
sure in faith, strong in hope, perfected in love.
And when our earthly journey is ended,
lead us rejoicing into your kingdom,
where you live for ever and ever.
R. Amen.

V. Eternal rest grant unto them, O Lord,
R. and let perpetual light shine upon them.

V. May they rest in peace.
R. Amen.

V. May their souls and the souls of all the faithful departed, through the mercy of God, rest
in peace.
R. Amen.

All make the Sign of the Cross as the leader concludes:

May the peace of God,
which is beyond all understanding,
keep our hearts and minds
in the knowledge and love of God
and of his Son, our Lord Jesus Christ.
R. Amen.[29]

Prayer to the Sacred Heart of Our Lord for Ourselves, Our Friends, and the Souls in Purgatory

By St. Margaret Mary Alacoque

I have placed all my confidence in Thee, do not reject me. I call Thee, I invoke Thee as the sovereign
remedy for all my evils, the greatest of which is sin.
Destroy it in me and grant me pardon for all the
sins that I have committed, of which I repent with
my whole heart, and ask your forgiveness for them.

Make then Thy sovereign power, O loving
Heart, felt by me and by all hearts capable of loving you, especially my parents and friends, and by
all those persons who have recommended themselves to my prayers for whom I have a special

obligation. Assist them, I beseech Thee, according to their necessities.

O Heart full of charity, soften hardened hearts and relieve the souls in Purgatory; be the assured refuge of those in their last agony and the consolation of all those who are afflicted or in need. In time, O Heart of Love, be to all in all things; but especially at the hour of my death, be the safe retreat for my poor bewildered soul. At that moment, receive it into the bosom of Thy mercy. Amen.

St. Frances Xavier Cabrini

(November 13)

A Prayer for Peace of Mind
By St. Frances Xavier Cabrini

Fortify me with the grace of your Holy Spirit and give your peace to my soul that I may be free from all needless anxiety, solicitude, and worry. Help me to desire always that which is pleasing and acceptable to you so that your will may be my will. Grant that I may rid myself of all unholy desires and that, for your love, I may remain obscure and unknown in this world, to be known only to you. Do not permit me to attribute to myself the good that you perform in me and through me, but rather, referring all honor to your Majesty, may I glory only in my infirmities, so that renouncing sincerely all vainglory which comes from the world, I may aspire to that true and lasting glory which comes from you. Amen.

God, our Father, you called Frances Xavier Cabrini from Italy to serve the immigrants of America. By her example teach us concern for the stranger, the sick and the frustrated. By her prayers help us to see Christ in all the men and women we meet. Grant this through our Lord Jesus Christ, your Son, who lives and reigns with you and the Holy Spirit, one God, for ever and ever.

Amen.

Bl. Miguel Pro

(November 23)

Does our life become from day to day more painful, more oppressive, more replete with afflictions? Blessed be He a thousand times who desires it so. If life be harder, love makes it also stronger, and only this love, grounded on suffering, can carry the Cross of my Lord Jesus Christ. Love without egotism, without relying on self, but enkindling in the depth of the heart an ardent thirst to love and suffer for all those around us: a thirst that neither misfortune nor contempt can extinguish....

I believe, O Lord; but strengthen my faith ...

Heart of Jesus, I love Thee; but increase my love.

Heart of Jesus, I trust in Thee; but give
greater vigor to my confidence.

Heart of Jesus, I give my heart to Thee; but
so enclose it in Thee that it may never be
separated from Thee.

Heart of Jesus, I am all Thine; but take care
of my promise so that I may be able to
put it in practice even unto the complete
sacrifice of my life.

*(Bl. Miguel Pro, 1891-1927, Mexican Jesuit who
ministered to the Mexican people despite government
prohibition, was unjustly accused of an assassination plot
against the president, and was arrested and executed.)*

Thanksgiving Day

(Fourth Thursday in November)
*This prayer may be used at the family dinner table
with one of the blessings of the table and a Scripture
reading (for example, Philippians 4:4-7).*

Lord, we thank you
for the goodness of our people
and for the spirit of justice
that fills this nation.
We thank you for the beauty and fullness of the
land and the challenge of the cities.

We thank you for our work and our rest,
for one another, and for our homes.

We thank you, Lord:
accept our thanksgiving on this day.
We pray and give thanks through Jesus Christ
    our Lord.
R. Amen.[30]

Immaculate Conception

(December 8)

O God, who by the Immaculate Conception of
    the Blessed Virgin
prepared a worthy dwelling for your Son,
grant, we pray, that as you preserved her from
    every stain
by virtue of the Death of your Son, which you
    foresaw,
so, through her intercession,
we, too, may be cleansed and admitted to your
    presence.[31]

*(This feast celebrates Mary, conceived without sin.
She is the patron of Catholics in the United States.)*

Our Lady of Guadalupe

(December 12)

God of power and mercy,
you blessed the Americas at Tepeyac
with the presence of the Virgin Mary of
    Guadalupe.
May her prayers help all men and women
to accept each other as brothers and sisters.

Through your justice present in our hearts
may your peace reign in the world.

Grant this through Christ our Lord.
R. Amen.

*(Our Lady appeared to St. Juan Diego near Mexico
City in 1531 and left her image on his cloak. She is
patron of the Americas and speaks for the poor and
oppressed.)*

SPECIAL OCCASIONS

St. Thérèse of Lisieux remarked: "For me, prayer is a surge of the heart; it is a simple look turned toward heaven, it is a cry of recognition and of love, embracing both trial and joy."¹ We must remember to pray in good times and in bad, for such is the reality of life.

BLESSING AND THANKSGIVING

Blessing in Times of Joy and Thanksgiving

All make the Sign of the Cross. The leader begins:

Give praise to God, who is rich in mercy and who has favored us in wonderful ways. Blessed be God now and for ever.

All respond: Amen.

The leader may use these or similar words to introduce the blessing:

St. Paul teaches us to give thanks to God the Father always through Christ, in whom he has given us everything.

Then the Scripture is read:

Listen to the words of the apostle Paul to the Philippians: *(Read Philippians 4:4-7 [alternate readings: Colossians 3:15-17 or 1 Thessalonians 5:12-24].)*

The reader concludes: The Word of the Lord.
All respond: Thanks be to God.

After a time of silence, all join in prayers of intercession and in the Lord's Prayer. Then the leader prays:

Almighty Father,
you are lavish in bestowing all your gifts,
and we give you thanks for the favors you have
    given to us.
In your goodness you have favored us
and kept us safe in the past.
We ask that you continue to protect us
and to shelter us in the shadow of your wings.

We ask this through Christ our Lord.

All respond: Amen.

All make the Sign of the Cross as the leader concludes:

May God the Father, with the Son and the Holy
    Spirit,
who has shown us such great mercy,
be praised and blessed for ever and ever.

All respond: Amen.[2]

Prayer of Thanks for One's Home

Most Blessed Trinity —
Father, Son and Holy Spirit —
    we give thanks for the great blessings
    bestowed upon all who live in this house.

May all who reside here and all who visit
    continue to feel the warmth of the love
    that flows through faith and trust in you.

Protect our home from storms and fire
    and all kinds of danger.
Keep us from sin.
Keep us in your love.

Holy Immaculate Mother of God
    and Glorious St. Joseph,
    protectors and patrons of our homes,
    save and protect us now
    and at the hour of our death.
Amen.[3]

Thanksgiving for a Safe Return

Praise to you, O Lord, for our safe return.
In your great mercy,
continue to guide and protect us
and keep us safe.
Amen.

Prayer on Graduation Day

Lord Jesus, you have said that your followers
    must be the light of the world.
Light propagates itself,
    dispels darkness.
It sows rays of joy and hope.
It is life-giving.
Help me, Lord, to be a light to this world,
    so that my life radiates your message of
    love, hope, and joy.
May I be the beacon leading
    to you those who seek truth.

You also said, Lord Jesus,
    that your disciples must be
    the salt to this earth.
Lord, may I be the salt
    that takes away the blandness
    in the routine of living,
    that prevents the rottenness
    of hatred and greed from expanding,

that brings compassionate healing
to anguished souls I encounter.

"Be the leaven to the world,"
    said you to your friends.
Bread, a staple of life,
    and cakes, always present at celebrations,
    would be dull and lifeless without the
    tiny bit of yeast.
Teach me, Lord Jesus,
    that alone I am insignificant,
    but mixed with the talents of
    my brothers and sisters,
    I can lift this world out of
    its insipid mediocrity.
May I be a bit of leaven in the
    Bread of Life,
    and a sign of your celebration
    in this life and life eternal.

Lord, let this be a beginning of my life.
In the days of darkness, be my Light,
    so that in turn I can radiate your
    truth and your message of love,
    hope, and joy.
In the days of blandness,
    Lord, be my Salt,
    so that in turn I can fend off the
    corruption, the staleness and
    mediocrity around me.

In the days when I am flat on my back
    or fall flat on my face,
        Lord, be my Leaven, so that not only
        can I rise again,
        but also raise the downhearted to the
        celebration of your Love.
And Lord, thank you,
    for the school years and talents
        I have received. Amen.[4]

In Praise of God's Grandeur

By St. Catherine of Siena

Dear Lord,
it seems that you are so madly in love
    with your creatures that
        you could not live without us.
So you created us;
    and then, when we turned away from you,
        you redeemed us.
Yet, you are God and so have no need of us.
Your greatness is made no greater by our
        creation;
    your power is made no stronger by our
        redemption.
You have no duty to care for us,
    no debt to repay us.
It is love, and love alone, which moves you.[5]

PETITION AND INTERCESSION

Prayers for Traveling or Vacations

While waiting for traffic, a quick "Jesus, Mary, and Joseph" can help bring needed patience and calm. Long trips are ideal times for praying the Rosary or learning a new prayer. Many simply pray: "St. Christopher, protect us. Guardian angel, protect us," before each journey. When a vehicle is stopped on the side of the road, it would be an act of kindness to pray that the people keep safe and arrive at their destination.

Prayer for Motorists

By Pope St. John XXIII

O God, Almighty Father, who has created man in your image and has infused in his body an immortal soul that yearns and desires to come to you through the ways of faith, to rest in you, grant that we, engaged in driving along the roads of this world may be always mindful of our grave responsibility, and do show us the way of charity and prudence.

O Jesus, Incarnate Word, who while here did travel the earth's roads to free your enemies, to heal the sick and to preach the kingdom of heaven, keep us and strengthen us always in your grace.

Immaculate Virgin, who did sustain the Child Jesus on the road to exile and did accompany Him on His boyhood journeys to the Holy City, and were close to Him on His way to Calvary, but now assumed into heaven, you, Goodness and Mercy, Road and Gate of Heaven, protect us in our earthly journeys, defend us from all dangers of soul and body to which we are continually exposed; make us kind and patient to those who trust themselves to our care.

Heavenly angels, messengers of the Most High, saints of heaven, obtain for us such a lively faith that we may direct our life to God and be always ready for the last journey home, where with you we shall praise God forever and ever.

Amen.

(Pope John XXIII reigned as pope from 1958 to 1963, during which he convoked the Second Vatican Council, which renewed the life of the Church. He was declared a saint April 27, 2014. Feast: October 11.)

Motorist Prayer

Lord, protect me, my passengers and all who I pass by with a steady hand and a watchful eye.

Prayer Before Leaving on a Journey
All make the Sign of the Cross. The leader begins:

May the Lord turn his face toward us and guide our feet into the way of peace, now and for ever.
All respond: Amen.

The leader may use these or similar words to introduce the blessing:

Let us entrust those who are leaving to the hands of the Lord. Let us pray that he will give them a prosperous journey and that as they travel they will praise him in all his creatures; that they will experience God's own goodness in the hospitality they receive and bring the Good News of salvation to all those they meet; that they will be courteous toward all; that they will greet the poor and afflicted with kindness and know how to comfort and help them.

Then the Scripture is read:

Listen to the words of the Book of Tobit: (*Read Tobit 5:17b-18a, 21-22 [alternate readings: Genesis 28:10-16 or Deuteronomy 6:4-9].)*

The reader concludes: The Word of the Lord.
All respond: Thanks be to God.

After a time of silence, all join in prayers of interces-sion and in the Lord's Prayer. Then the leader prays:

All-powerful and merciful God,
you led the children of Israel on dry land,
    parting the waters of the sea;
you guided the Magi to your Son by a star.
Help our brother/sister, N., (Or: Help our
    brothers/sisters, N. and N.) and give him/
    her (them) a safe journey.
Under your protection let him/her (them)
reach his/her (their) destination
and come at last to the eternal haven of
    salvation.

We ask this through Christ our Lord.
R. Amen.

If all are making the journey, the leader prays:

All-powerful and ever-living God,
when Abraham left his own land
and departed from his own people,
you kept him safe all through his journey.
Protect us, who also are your servants:
walk by our side to help us;
be our companion and our strength on the road
and our refuge in every adversity.
Lead us, O Lord,

so that we will reach our destination in safety
and happily return to our home(s).

We ask this through Christ our Lord.
R. Amen.

All make the Sign of the Cross as the leader concludes:
May God bless you with every heavenly blessing
and give you a safe journey;
wherever life leads you,
may you find him there to protect you.

We ask this through Christ our Lord.
R. Amen.

Or:

May almighty God bless us
and hear our prayers for a safe journey.
R. Amen.[6]

Prayer to Avert Storms

Let all the winds of evil be driven from our house,
we implore you, O Lord, and may the raging
tempests be subdued, through our Lord Jesus
Christ, your Son, who lives and reigns with you
in the unity of the Holy Spirit, world without
end. Amen.

258 | Special Occasions

A Prayer for Rain

O God, heavenly Father,
who by thy Son, Jesus Christ,
has promised to all those who seek thy
    kingdom,
all things necessary to their bodily sustenance:
Send us, we beseech thee,
in this our necessity,
such moderate rain and showers
that we may receive the fruits of the earth
to our comfort and to your honor.
Through Jesus Christ our Lord.
Amen.

Prayer for Welcoming Guests

May grace be yours
and peace in abundance from God,
now and for ever.
R. Amen.

Prayer for Those We Love

By St. Ambrose of Milan

Lord God, we can hope for others nothing better than the happiness we desire for ourselves. Therefore, I pray you, do not separate me after death from those I tenderly loved on earth. Grant that where I am they may be with me, and that I may enjoy their presence in heaven after being so often deprived of it on earth. Lord God, I ask you to receive your beloved children immediately into your life-giving heart. After this brief life on earth, give them eternal happiness.

Amen.[7]

(St. Ambrose, 339-397, bishop of Milan, a gifted writer and homilist, was proclaimed Father and Doctor of the Church. Feast: December 7.)

Prayer for Friends

(An old French Prayer)

Blessed Mother of those whose names you can read in my heart, watch over them with every care. Make their way easy and their labors fruitful. Dry their tears if they weep; sanctify their joys; raise their courage if they weaken; restore their hope if they lose heart, their health if they be ill, truth if they err, and repentance if they fall.

Amen.

Prayer for One's Enemies

By St. Thomas More

Almighty God, have mercy on N. and on all that
bear me evil will and would do me harm, and
on their faults and mine together, by such easy,
tender, merciful means, as thine infinite wisdom
best can devise; vouchsafe to amend and redress
and make us saved souls in heaven together, where
we may ever live and love together with thee and
thy blessed saints. O glorious Trinity, for the bitter
passion of our sweet Savior Christ.

Amen.

Prayer for Mercy

By Thomas à Kempis

Take away, O Lord, from our hearts all suspi-
ciousness, indignation, anger, and contention, and
whatever is calculated to wound charity, and to
lessen brotherly love.

Have mercy, O Lord, have mercy on those who
seek thy mercy; give grace to the needy; make us
so to live, that we may be found worthy to enjoy
the fruition of thy grace, and that we may attain
to eternal life.

Serenity Prayer

God, grant me the serenity to accept the things
    I cannot change,
Courage to change the things I can,
And wisdom to know the difference.

For Prudence in Speech

O Lord, place a guard upon my tongue and discretion upon my lips that my conversation may be modest, charitable, and truthful. Amen.

Prayer in Times of Seeking God's Will

Psalm 27:7-9, 13-14

Hear, O LORD, when I cry aloud,
    be gracious to me and answer me!
You have said, "Seek my face."
    My heart says to you,
"Your face, LORD, do I seek."
    Hide not your face from me....

I believe that I shall see the goodness of the
    LORD
    in the land of the living!
Wait for the LORD;
    be strong, and let your heart take courage;
    yes, wait for the LORD! (RSV-SCE)

Prayer for a Holy Heart

By St. Thomas More

Lord, grant me a holy heart that sees always what is fine and pure and is not frightened at the sight of sin, but creates order wherever it goes.

Grant me a heart that knows nothing of boredom, weeping, and sighing.

Let me not be too concerned with the bothersome thing I call "myself."

Lord, give me a sense of humor and I will find happiness in life and profit for others.

Prayer for Those in Military Service

O Prince of Peace, we humbly ask your
    protection
for all our men and women in military service.
Give them unflinching courage to defend
with honor, dignity, and devotion,
the rights of all who are imperiled
by injustice and evil.
Be their rock, their shield, and their stronghold
and let them draw their strength from you.
For you are God, forever and ever.[8]

Irish Blessing

May the road rise up to meet you,
May the wind be ever at your back.
May the sun shine warm upon your face
And the rain fall softly on your fields.
And until we meet again,
May God hold you in the hollow of His hand.

Prayers to One's Patron Saint

O heavenly Patron, whose name I have the honor
to bear, pray earnestly at all times to God for me,
confirm me in the faith; strengthen me in virtue,
defend me in the battle of life; so that, conquer-
ing the enemy of my soul, I may deserve to be
rewarded with everlasting glory.
Amen.

Patron, whose name I bear, be mindful of me before God. Pray for me that I may always live as I
ought, that I may keep the faith and be victorious
in the battle of life.
Amen.[9]

Prayer for Guidance

By St. Thomas Aquinas

Grant to me, O Lord, my God,
That I may not falter in times of prosperity or
    adversity. Amen.

Prayer for Justice and Peace

By Pope Pius XII

Almighty and eternal God,
May your grace enkindle in all of us a love for
    the many unfortunate people whom poverty
    and misery reduce to a condition of life
    unworthy of human beings.
Arouse in the hearts of those who call you
    Father a hunger and thirst for justice and
    peace, and for fraternal charity in deeds and
    in truth.
Grant, O Lord, peace in our days, peace to
    souls, peace to families, peace to our
    country, and peace among nations. Amen.[10]

Prayer for Peace

By Henri J. M. Nouwen

Dear God,
with you everything is possible.
Let the cup of war,
killing, and destruction,

the cup of bloodshed,
human anguish and desolation,
the cup of torture,
breakage in human relationships and
    abandonment ...
Dear God,
let this cup pass us by. Amen.[11]

Act of Consecration for the United States

Most Holy Trinity — Father, Son and Holy Spirit — in union with the Blessed Virgin Mary, we adore Your majesty and acknowledge Your supreme eternal dominion and authority.

Most Holy Trinity, we place the United States of America into the hands of Mary Immaculate in order that she may present the country to You. Through the intercession of Mary, have mercy on our President and on all the officers of our government. Protect family life in our nation. Grant the precious gift of many vocations to the priesthood and religious life. Have mercy on the sick, the poor, the tempted, and all who are in need.

Mary, Immaculate Virgin, Our Mother, Patroness of our land, we honor you and ask your maternal protection and care for us. Obtain for us the graces we need to live and die according to the Will of your Divine Son. Amen.

—————— FAMILY PRAYERS ——————

Prayers for Our Family

Almighty Father,

We give You thanks for the gift of Your Son, who saved us through the wood of the cross. We give You thanks for all the favors we received through Jesus Christ, our Lord, the intercession of His Blessed Mother and all the saints. We commend our family to Your fatherly protection; heal the wounds of those who suffer, comfort the sick and those who are alone, and keep all of us in Your love and peace.

Lord Jesus, through Your cross,
   help us carry ours.
Holy Mary, Mother of grace and mercy,
   intercede for us.
St. Joseph, Guardian of the Holy Family,
   watch over us.
St. Theresa, St. Jude, and all the saints,
   pray for us.
Amen.[12]

Lord, bless our family, all of us now together, those far away, all who are gone back to you. May we know joy. May we bear our sorrows in patience. Let love guide our understanding of each other. Let us be grateful to each other. We have all made each other what we are. O Family of Jesus, watch over our family.

Amen.[13]

———

Blessed St. Joseph, holy guardian of Jesus and Mary, assist us by your prayers in all necessities of life. Ask of Jesus that special grace which He granted to you, to watch over our home at the pillow of the sick and the dying, so that with Mary and with you, heaven may find our family unbroken in the Sacred Heart of Jesus. Amen.

———

O dear Jesus, I humbly implore you
to grant your special graces to our family.
May our home be a shrine of peace,
purity, love, labor, and faith.
I beg you, dear Jesus, to protect and bless
all of us, absent and present,
living and dead. Amen.[14]

Prayer to St. Joseph

St. Joseph, you are the chaste and loving spouse of the Virgin Mary, the foster father of Jesus, the provider and protector of the Holy Family and of all families. We have complete confidence in your loving care for new life and in your fidelity to the family. Despise not our prayer, but graciously hear us. Amen.

Prayer of Spouses for Each Other

Lord Jesus, grant that I and my spouse may have a true and understanding love for each other. Grant that we may both be filled with faith and trust. Give us the grace to live with each other in peace and harmony. May we always bear with one another's weaknesses and grow from each other's strengths. Help us to forgive one another's failings and grant us patience, kindness, cheerfulness, and the spirit of placing the well-being of one another ahead of self.

May the love that brought us together grow and mature with each passing year. Bring us both ever closer to You through our love for each other. Let our love grow to perfection. Amen.

Prayer for a Wedding Anniversary

Lord, our God and Father, in the beginning you created man and woman to be united in the bond of marriage. Bless and strengthen our love that our life together may be an ever truer reflection of the union between Christ and his Church.

Through Christ our Lord.

Amen.[15]

Prayer for Expectant Parents

Father, we thank you for your marvelous gift; you have allowed us to share in your divine parenthood.

During this time of waiting, we ask you to protect and nurture these first mysterious stirrings of life. May our child come safely into the light of the world and to the new birth of baptism.

Mother of God, we entrust our child to your loving heart.

Amen.[16]

Parent's Prayer for Children

O Jesus, Lover of children,
    bestow your most precious graces
    on those whom you have confided to our
       care.
Increase in them Faith, Hope, and Charity.

May your love lead them to solid piety,
    inspiring them with dread for sin,
    love for work and an ardent desire
    of worthily approaching your Holy Table.

Preserve in them innocence and purity of heart;
    and if they should offend you,
    grant them the grace of a prompt and sincere
      repentance.

From your tabernacle
    watch over them day and night;
    protect them in all their ways.

Grant that they may acquire the knowledge
    that they need to embrace the state of life
    to which you have called them.

Grant us a sincere love,
    constant vigilance
    and generous devotedness towards them.

Grant us all consolation on earth
    and eternal reward in heaven.

A Parent's Prayer to St. Monica

St. Monica, patron of Christian mothers, we entrust to your protection the children whose names you can read in our hearts. Pray for them that they may be granted strength to combat weakness, victory over temptation, guidance to resolve their doubts, and success in all their undertakings. May they enjoy good health of mind and body, see beauty and worth in all created things, and serve the Lord with firm faith, joyful hope, and enduring love.

    Amen.

Daily Blessing of a Child

Make the Sign of the Cross on the child's forehead and pray one of these blessings:

- May God bless you.
- May God keep you safe.
- God be with you.
- God be in your heart.
- May God bless and protect you.

Blessing on a Birthday

Father in heaven, _____ years ago today, you blessed me with N., as my daughter/son. I ask you now to bless N. on his/her birthday and to keep him/her in Your care, now and in the coming year.

Child responds: **Amen.**

Blessings for Times of Sickness

God of love,
ever caring,
ever strong,
stand by us in our time of need.

Watch over your child N. who is sick;
look after him/her in every danger,
and grant him/her your healing and peace.

We ask this in the name of Jesus the Lord.
R. Amen.[17]

———

- May God be with you now and bring you to good health.
- May God give you a complete recovery.
- May God give you strength and peace.

(Note: If someone is seriously ill, a priest should be notified so that the person can receive the sacrament of the Anointing of the Sick.)

Blessings for Safety

Lord God, may you be with N. and protect him/her this day.

Child responds: **Amen.**

May the Lord give my son/daughter His merciful protection this day, and may Our Lady cover you with her mantle.

Child responds: **Amen.**

May the Lord be with you and protect you and send His holy angels to surround you to guard you.

Child responds: **Amen.**

Prayer for Our Youth

God, our Father,
we thank you for the gift of love
   and the gift of life.

We thank you for the gift of our children.

We ask you to send your holy angels
   to protect and guide them each day
   so that they will walk the narrow path of
      purity,
   self-control and obedience,
   as was taught to us by your own Son,
   Jesus Christ.

We ask this through Jesus Christ our Lord,
   in union with the Holy Spirit.
Amen.

Our Lady of Guadalupe … pray for our youth.
St. Michael … pray for our youth.
St. Charles Borromeo … pray for our youth.

Prayer to St. John, Patron of Caregivers

Beloved St. John, from the cross Jesus entrusted to you the care of His Blessed Mother. Help me and all those taking care of a loved one who is sick, elderly, disabled, or frail. Pray for us, that as we go about our many caregiving duties, we may never lose sight of that truth which Christ revealed to

His disciples: "Whatever you did for one of these, you did for Me." Amen.[18]

A Prayer for Teachers

By Cardinal Richard J. Cushing

Heavenly Father, Who promised that all those who instruct others in the ways of holiness will shine as stars for all eternity, fill our hearts and minds with true knowledge and the art of teaching. Give us patience and understanding, justice and prudence, humility and fear of the Lord. Grant us wisdom and charity so that with a pure and holy love of God we ourselves may enjoy all these gifts and impart them to our students.

Teach our children to be obedient to Your laws and open to Your inspiration. Let them be instruments of Your peace in their homes, in our land, and in the family of nations as becomes children of the sons of God in the Mystical Body of Christ.

May the blessings of Your seven-fold gifts be in all who teach and in all who learn through the Holy Spirit, Who is the Love of the Father and the Son, Our Lord Jesus Christ — The Divine Teacher.

Amen.

(Cardinal Richard J. Cushing, 1895-1970, was archbishop of Boston and one of the most respected leaders of the Catholic Church.)

—— SUFFERING AND TRIALS ——

Healing Prayer

Jesus, I ask you to enter into my heart and release me from those life experiences that torment me. You know me so much better than I know myself. Therefore, bring your love to every corner of my heart. Wherever you discover the wounded child, touch, console, and release me.

Walk back through my life to the very moment when I was conceived. Cleanse my bloodlines and free me from those things which may have exerted a negative influence at that moment. Bless me again as I was being formed within my mother's womb and remove all barriers to wholeness which may have affected me during those months of confinement. Bridge the gap between the love that I needed and never perceived receiving.

Jesus, I ask you to surround my infancy with your light and heal those memories which keep me from being free. If I needed more of a mother's love, send me your Mother, Mary, to provide whatever was lacking. If I needed more of a father's love and security to assure me that I was wanted and loved very deeply, I ask you to hold me and let me feel your strong, protective arms. Give me renewed confidence and courage to face the trials of the world because I know my Father's love will support me if I stumble and fall.

Thank you, Lord![19]

Prayer in Time of Sickness

O Jesus, You suffered and died for us;
You understand suffering;
Teach me to understand my suffering as You do;
To bear it in union with You;
To offer it with You to atone for my sins
And to bring Your grace to souls in need.
Calm my fears; increase my trust,
May I gladly accept Your holy will and become
  more like You in trial.
If it be Your will, restore me to health so that I
  may work for Your honor and glory and the
  salvation of all.
Amen.

Prayer to the Divine Physician

Dear Jesus, Divine Physician and Healer of the
Sick, we turn to you in this time of illness. O
dearest Comforter of the Troubled, alleviate our
worry and sorrow with your gentle love, and grant
us the grace and strength to accept this burden.
Dear God, we place our worries in your hands.
We place our sick under your care and humbly
ask that you restore your servant to health again.
Above all, grant us the grace to acknowledge your
holy will and know that whatsoever you do, you
do for the love of us.
  Amen.[20]

Prayer for the Despairing

O God, you care for your creation with great tenderness. In the midst of overwhelming pain, you offer hope. Give help to me, whose spirit seems to be lost and whose soul is in despair. Let me feel your love. Let me believe in a rebirth of joy so that I can experience now a small taste of the happiness I wish to know in eternity.[21]

(This prayer was written by a seventh-century Irish monk, Dimma.)

Prayer for the Sick

Father,
your Son accepted our sufferings
to teach us the virtue of patience in human
     illness.
Hear the prayers we offer for our sick brother/
     sister.
May all who suffer pain, illness, or disease
realize that they have been chosen to be saints
and know that they are joined to Christ
in his suffering for the salvation of the world.

We ask this through Christ our Lord.
R. Amen.[22]

Prayer of Support for the Sick

Father in heaven, grant N. comfort in his/her suffering. Give him/her courage when afraid, patience when afflicted, hope when dejected and when alone assure him/her of the prayerful support of your holy people. We ask this through Christ our Lord.

Amen.[23]

Blessing of the Sick

All make the Sign of the Cross. The leader begins:

Let us bless the Lord, who went about doing good and healing the sick. Blessed be God now and for ever.

All respond: Blessed be God now and for ever.

Scripture Reading. Read Romans 12:1-2 or Matthew 15:29-31. The reader concludes:

The Word of the Lord.

All respond: Thanks be to God.

After a time of silence, all join in prayers of intercession and the Lord's Prayer. The leader and others present may wish to make the Sign of the Cross on the forehead of the one who is sick or simply place a hand on the person during the prayer:

Lord and Father, almighty and eternal God,
by your blessing you give us strength and
    support in our frailty:
turn with kindness toward this your servant N.
Free him/her from all illness and restore him/
    her to health,
so that in the sure knowledge of your goodness
he/she will gratefully bless your holy name.

We ask this through Christ our Lord.
R. Amen.

All make the Sign of the Cross as the leader concludes:

May the Lord Jesus Christ,
who went about doing good and healing the
    sick,
grant that we may have good health
and be enriched by his blessings.
R. Amen.[24]

Short Prayers for Those Who Are Sick

*Those who are sick may use brief prayers, repeated
slowly over and over:*

- Lord Jesus Christ, Son of the living God, have
  mercy on me.
- Praised be Jesus Christ.
- Lord, I hope in you.

- Your will be done.
- Strengthen me, Lord.
- Lord, have mercy.
- Sacred Heart of Jesus, have mercy on us.
- My Lord and my God.
- Jesus, Mary, and Joseph.
- Pray for us, holy Mother of God, that we may become worthy of the promises of Christ.
- Holy Mary, pray for us.

Prayer to St. Gerard for a Sick Child

St. Gerard, who, like our Divine Savior, showed such loving tenderness to children and delivered so many from disease and even from death, graciously look upon us now weighed down with sorrow. We implore you by your prayers to restore our child to health, if such be the holy will of God. We promise to bring him/her up a good Christian and to safeguard him/her by constant watchfulness from all contagion of sin. We implore this favor, O compassionate Brother through the love with which Jesus and Mary surrounded your own childhood. Amen.

(St. Gerard Majella, 1725-1755, Italian Redemptorist lay brother, is known for his miracles on behalf of the poor, families, mothers and children, and those making a good confession. Patron of mothers. Feast: October 16.)

A Caregiver's Prayer

Heavenly Father, help me better understand
and believe I can do what you ask me to do.

Forgive me for the times, even now,
when I question your judgment.

As I go about the many daily tasks of
    caregiving,
give me energy.

As I watch my loved one oh-so-slowly walk
across the room, give me strength.

As I answer his/her repeated question
just one more time, give me patience.

As I look for solutions to whatever
is the most recent concern, give me wisdom.
As I reminisce with him/her about the
"good old days," give me a moment of laughter.

As I get to know my loved one in a new way,
seeing both his/her strength and frailty, give me
    joy.

As I sit beside my loved one's bed waiting
for his/her pain medication to take effect,
give me comfort.

Lighten my burden, answer my prayer,
and give me the strength to do what
so often seems impossible.

Give me a quiet place to rest when I need it
and a quieting of my anxieties when I'm there.

Change my attitude from a tired,
frustrated and angry caregiver
to the loving and compassionate
one I want to be.

Remain my constant companion as I face
the challenges of caregiving
and when my job is through
and it's time for me to let go,
help me remember
he/she is leaving my loving arms
to enter your eternal embrace. Amen.[25]

—— PRAYERS FOR THE DYING ——

Scripture Readings for the Dying

The following texts may be prayed with or for the dying:

Revelation 21:1-7

Then I saw a new heaven and a new earth; for the
first heaven and the first earth had passed away,
and the sea was no more. And I saw the holy city,

new Jerusalem, coming down out of heaven from God, prepared as a bride adorned for her husband; and I heard a great voice from the throne saying, "Behold, the dwelling of God is with men. He will dwell with them, and they shall be his people, and God himself will be with them; he will wipe away every tear from their eyes, and death shall be no more, neither shall there be mourning nor crying nor pain any more, for the former things have passed away."

And he who sat upon the throne said, "Behold, I make all things new." Also he said, "Write this, for these words are trustworthy and true." And he said to me, "It is done! I am the Alpha and the Omega, the beginning and the end. To the thirsty I will give water without price from the fountain of the water of life. He who conquers shall have this heritage, and I will be his God and he shall be my son."

Romans 14:8

If we live, we live to the Lord, and if we die, we die to the Lord; so then, whether we live or whether we die, we are the Lord's.

John 6:37-40

All that the Father gives me will come to me; and him who comes to me I will not cast out. For I have come down from heaven, not to do my own will, but the will of him who sent me; and this is the will of him who sent me, that I should lose nothing of all that he has given me, but raise it up at the last day. For this is the will of my Father, that every one who sees the Son and believes in him should have eternal life; and I will raise him up at the last day.

1 Thessalonians 4:17

Then we who are alive, who are left, shall be caught up together with them in the clouds to meet the Lord in the air; and so we shall always be with the Lord.

Optional Scripture Readings

Job 19:23-27; Ps 23; Ps 25; Ps 91; Ps 121; 1 Jn 4:16; Mt 25:1-13; Lk 22:39-46; Lk 23:44-49; Lk 24:1-8; Jn 14:6, 23, 27.

Short Readings: Rom 8:35; Ps 25:1; Ps 23:4; Ps 31:5a; Lk 23:42; Acts 7:59.[26]

Prayer to St. Joseph for a Happy Death

O Blessed Joseph, who died in the arms of Jesus and Mary, obtain for me, I beseech you, the grace of a happy death. In that hour of dread and anguish, assist me by your presence, and protect me by your power against the enemies of my salvation. Into your sacred hands, living and dying, Jesus, Mary, Joseph, I commend my soul. Amen.

(St. Joseph is said to have had the privilege of dying in the arms of Jesus and Mary and is the patron of a happy death.)

Prayer for a Peaceful Death

Jesus, Mary, and Joseph, I give you my heart
    and soul,
Jesus, Mary, and Joseph, assist me in my last
    agony.
Jesus, Mary, and Joseph, let me breathe forth
    my spirit in peace with you.

Prayers of Commendation

As the time of death approaches, this prayer may be said:

Go forth, Christian soul, from this world
in the name of God the almighty Father,
who created you,
in the name of Jesus Christ, Son of the Living
    God,
who suffered for you,
in the name of the Holy Spirit,
who was poured out upon you,
go forth, faithful Christian.

May you live in peace this day,
may your home be with God in Zion,
with Mary, the virgin Mother of God,
with Joseph, and all the angels and saints.[27]

— Prayers for the Deceased —

It is an ancient and pious practice of the Church to pray for the dead. St. John Chrysostom advised: "Let us help and commemorate them. If Job's sons were purified by their father's sacrifice, why would we doubt that our offerings for the dead bring them some consolation? Let us not hesitate to help those who have died and to offer our prayers for them."

Prayers After Death

Saints of God, come to his/her aid!
Come to meet him/her, angels of the Lord!
R. Receive his/her soul and present him/her to
    God the Most High.
May Christ, who called you, take you to himself;
    may angels lead you to Abraham's side. **R.**
Give him/her eternal rest, O Lord, and may
    your light shine on him/her for ever. **R.**

Let us pray.
All-powerful and merciful God,
we commend to you N., your servant.
In your mercy and love,
blot out the sins he/she has committed
through human weakness.
In this world he/she has died:
let him/her live with you for ever.
We ask this through Christ our Lord.
R. Amen.

These verses may also be used:

V. Eternal rest grant unto him/her, O Lord.

R. And let perpetual light shine upon him/her.

V. May he/she rest in peace.

R. Amen.

V. May his/her soul and the souls of all the
   faithful departed,
      through the mercy of God,
      rest in peace.

R. Amen.[28]

In Paradisum (Into Paradise)

May God the Father look on you with love,
and call you to himself in bliss above.
May God the Son, good Shepherd of the sheep,
stretch out his hand and waken you from sleep.
May God the Spirit breathe on you his peace,
where joys beyond all knowing never cease.

May flights of angels lead you on your way,
to paradise, and heaven's eternal day!
May martyrs greet you after death's dark night,
and bid you enter into Zion's light!
May choirs of angels sing you to your rest
with once poor Lazarus, now forever blest.

*(In Paradisum is an antiphon from the traditional
Latin liturgy of the Western Church's Requiem Mass.
It is sung by the choir as the body is being taken out
of the church.)*

Preface from the Requiem Mass

It is truly right and just, our duty and our
    salvation,
always and everywhere to give you thanks,
Lord, holy Father, almighty and eternal God,
through Christ our Lord.

In him the hope of blessed resurrection has
    dawned,
that those saddened by the certainty of dying
might be consoled by the promise of
    immortality to come.
Indeed for your faithful, Lord,
life is changed not ended,
and, when this earthly dwelling turns to dust,
an eternal dwelling is made ready for them in
    heaven.

And so, with Angels and Archangels,
with Thrones and Dominions,
and with all the hosts and Powers of heaven,
we sing the hymn of your glory,
as without end we acclaim:

Holy, Holy, Holy Lord God of Hosts ...[29]

Prayer for a Deceased Relative or Friend

Father of Jesus,
by the merits of our blessed Savior,
look kindly on your servant _____,
who has died in the Catholic faith.
By the merits and prayers of Mary, the Mother
    of God,
St. Michael the Archangel and of all the saints,
may he/she rest in peace and rise to glory.
We ask this through Jesus Christ our Lord,
who lives and reigns with you,
in the unity of the Holy Spirit,
one God, for ever and ever. Amen.

*(Pray this prayer for a loved one for thirty days after
a funeral.)*

Prayer for the Souls in Purgatory

O gentle Heart of Jesus, ever present in the Blessed
Sacrament, ever consumed with burning love for
the poor captive souls in purgatory, have mercy
on them, especially _____.

Be not severe in your judgments, but let some of
your Precious Blood fall upon the devouring flames.

And, Merciful Savior, send your angels to conduct them to a place of refreshment, light and
peace. Amen.

*(Our Father. Hail Mary. Eternal rest grant unto them,
O Lord, and let perpetual light shine upon them.)*

Prayer for the Bereaved

Father,
God of all consolation,
in your unending love and mercy for us
you turn the darkness of death
into the dawn of new life.
Show compassion to your people in their sorrow.

Be our refuge and our strength
to lift us from the darkness of this grief
to the peace and light of your presence.

Your Son, our Lord Jesus Christ,
by dying for us, conquered death
and by rising again, restored life.

May we then go forward eagerly to meet him,
and after our life on earth
be reunited with our brothers and sisters
where every tear will be wiped away.

We ask this through Christ our Lord.
R. Amen.[30]

Prayers for Mourners

To be used by those in mourning:
Lord God,
you are attentive to the voice of our pleading.
Let us find in your Son
comfort in our sadness,

certainty in our doubt,
and courage to live through this hour.
Make our faith strong
through Christ our Lord.
R. Amen.[31]

For those who mourn the death of a child:
O Lord, whose ways are beyond understanding,
listen to the prayers of your faithful people:
that those weighed down by grief
at the loss of this [little] child
may we find reassurance in your infinite
     goodness.
We ask this through Christ our Lord.
R. Amen.[32]

CONSECRATIONS

Typical consecrations involve the giving or entrusting of oneself or one's family to Jesus or Mary with the desire for assistance in leading a virtuous life.

An Act of Consecration to Our Lady of the Miraculous Medal

All: O Virgin Mother of God, Mary Immaculate, we dedicate and consecrate ourselves to you under the title of Our Lady of the Miraculous Medal. May this Medal be for each one of us a sure sign of your affection for us and a constant reminder of our duties toward you. Ever while wearing it, may we be blessed by your loving protection and preserved in the grace of your Son. O Savior, keep us close to you every moment of our lives. Obtain for us, your children, the grace of a happy death; so that, in union with you, we may enjoy the bliss of heaven forever. Amen.

Leader: O Mary, conceived without sin.
All: Pray for us who have recourse to you *(three times)*.

Act of Consecration in the
Sacred Heart of Jesus

By St. Margaret Mary Alacoque

I give myself and consecrate to the Sacred Heart of our Lord Jesus Christ my person and my life, my actions, pains, and sufferings, so that I may be unwilling to make use of any part of my being other than to honor, love, and glorify the Sacred Heart. This is my unchanging purpose, namely, to be all His, and to do all things for the love of Him, at the same time renouncing with all my heart whatever is displeasing to Him. I therefore take you, O Sacred Heart, to be the only object of my love, the guardian of my life, my assurance of salvation, the remedy of my weakness and inconstancy, the atonement for all the faults of my life and my sure refuge at the hour of death. Be then, O Heart of goodness, my justification before God the Father, and turn away from me the strokes of His righteous anger.

O Heart of love, I put all my confidence in you, for I fear everything from my own wickedness and frailty, but I hope for all things from your goodness and bounty. Remove from me all that can displease you or resist your holy will; let your pure love imprint your image so deeply upon my heart, that I shall never be able to forget you or to be separated from you. May I obtain from all your loving kindness the grace of having my name written in your heart, for in you I desire to place all my happiness and glory, living and dying in bondage to you.[1]

Consecration to the Blessed Virgin

Hail Mary, …

My Queen! my Mother! I give you all of myself, and, to show my devotion to you, I consecrate to you my eyes, my ears, my mouth, my heart, my entire self. Therefore, O loving Mother, as I am your own, keep me, defend me, as your property and possession.

Consecration of the Family

Jesus, our most loving Redeemer, you came to enlighten the world with your teaching and example. You willed to spend the greater part of your life in humble obedience to Mary and Joseph in the poor home of Nazareth. In this way you sanctified that Family, which was to be an example for all Christian families.

Jesus, Mary, Joseph! Graciously accept our family which we dedicate and consecrate to you. Be pleased to protect, guard, and keep it in sincere faith, in peace and in the harmony of Christian charity. By conforming ourselves to the Divine model of your Family, may we all attain to eternal happiness.

Mary, Mother of Jesus and our Mother, by your merciful intercession make this our humble offering acceptable to Jesus, and obtain for us graces and blessings. St. Joseph, most holy guardian of Jesus and Mary, help us by your prayers in all our spiritual and temporal needs so that we may praise Jesus, our Divine Savior, together with Mary and you for all eternity.

PRAYERS FOR THE CHURCH AND THE WORLD

"The Church is a sacrament of salvation for all mankind…. The Church contributes to mankind's pilgrimage of conversion to God's plan through her witness and through such activities as dialogue, human promotion, commitment to justice and peace, education and the care of the sick, and aid to the poor and to children" (Pope St. John Paul II, *Redemptoris Missio*, n. 20).

Prayer for All

O Lord, Jesus Christ, hear my prayers for our Holy Father, our Bishop, our clergy, and for all who are in authority over us. Bless the whole Catholic Church, and turn all hearts toward your most merciful Heart. Bless my relatives, benefactors, friends and enemies. Help the poor, the sick, and those who are in their last agony. Have compassion on the souls in purgatory: grant them eternal rest and peace.

Amen.

Prayer for Christian Unity

(Ut unum sint)

Lord Jesus Christ, at your Last Supper you prayed
to the Father that all should be one. Send your
Holy Spirit upon all who hear your name and seek
to serve you. Strengthen our faith in you, and lead
us to love one another in humility. May we who
have been reborn in one baptism be united in one
faith under one Shepherd.

Amen.[1]

Prayer for Others

(From the Liturgy of St. John)

O Lord God of strength, who are true charity,
unshaken tranquility, and hope unfailing:

Do thou, O Lord our God, give to thy servants
here present in the sight of thy Majesty, the gifts
of charity, kindness, calmness, and lasting peace,
that we may all in purity of heart and goodness
of soul have peace with each other.

Prayers Attributed to
Pope St. Leo the Great

Against Error

O God, you who have established the foundations
of your Church upon the holy mountains: Grant
that she may not be moved by any wiles of error
which would fain compass her overthrow, nor may
she be shaken by any earthly disquietude, but ever

stand firmly upon the ordinances of the Apostles, and by their help, be kept in safety.

For Truth

O Lord: Give to your people, we pray you, the Spirit of Truth and of Peace, that they may know you with all their minds; and that, following with all their hearts after those things which are pleasing to you, they ever may possess the Gifts of your Bountiful Goodness.[2]

(St. Leo the Great was pope from 440 to 461 and is a Doctor of the Church. Feast: November 10.)

Prayers for the Pope

O God, who in your providential design
willed that your Church be built
upon blessed Peter, whom you set over the other
    Apostles,
look with favor, we pray, on N. our Pope
and grant that he, whom you have made Peter's
    successor,
may be for your people a visible source and
    foundation
of unity in faith and of communion.[3]

—•—

O God, shepherd and ruler of all the faithful,
look favorably on your servant N.,

whom you have set at the head of your Church
    as her shepherd;
grant, we pray, that by word and example
he may be of service to those over whom he
    presides
so that, together with the flock entrusted to his
    care,
he may come to everlasting life.[4]

Heavenly Father, guide and strengthen Pope N.,
chief pastor of your Church on earth.
May he by word and example
lead your people to eternal life.
Amen.

(It is a mark of Catholic unity to be devoted to the pope and to pray for him and his intentions regularly.)

Prayer for a Bishop

God, eternal shepherd, you tend your Church in many ways and rule us with love. You have chosen your servant N. to be a shepherd of your flock. Give him a spirit of courage and right judgment, a spirit of knowledge and love. By governing with fidelity those entrusted to his care, may he build your Church as a sign of salvation for the world.

Prayer for Priests

Lord Jesus, you have chosen your priests from among us and sent them out to proclaim your word and to act in your name. For so great a gift to your Church, we give you praise and thanksgiving. We ask you to fill them with the fire of your love, that their ministry may reveal your presence in the Church. Since they are earthen vessels, we pray that your power shine through their weakness. In their afflictions, let them never be crushed; in their doubts, never despair; in temptation, never be destroyed; in persecution, never abandoned. Inspire them through prayer to live each day the mystery of your dying and rising. In times of weakness send them your Spirit, and help them to praise your heavenly Father and to pray for poor sinners. By the same Holy Spirit, put your word on their lips and your love in their hearts, to bring good news to the poor and healing to the broken-hearted. And may the gift of Mary, your Mother, to the Disciple whom you loved, be your gift to every priest. Grant that she who formed you in her human image, may form them in your divine image, by the power of your Spirit, to the glory of God the Father.

Amen.[5]

Prayer for the Sanctification of the Clergy

Divine Savior, Jesus Christ, who has entrusted the whole work of your redemption, the welfare and salvation of the world, to priests as your representatives, I offer you through the hands of your most Holy Mother Mary, this present day, whole and entire, with all its prayers, works, and sacrifices, its joys and sorrows, for the sanctification of your priests, and for all those preparing for the priesthood. Give us truly holy priests, inflamed with the fire of your divine love, who seek nothing but your greater glory, and the salvation of souls. And you, Mary, good Mother of priests, protect all priests from dangers to their holy vocation, and with the loving hand of a mother, lead back to the Good Shepherd those unfortunate priests who, unfaithful to their exalted vocation, have gone astray. Amen.[6]

—— FOR VOCATIONS ——

Vatican II reminds, "In order to shepherd the People of God and to increase its numbers without cease, Christ the Lord set up in his Church a variety of offices which aim at the good of the whole body. The holders of office, who are invested with a sacred power, are, in fact, dedicated to promoting the interests of their brethren, so that all who belong to the People of God … may attain to salvation."[7]

Prayer by St. Charles Borromeo

O holy Mother of God, pray for the priests your Son has chosen to serve the Church. Help them, by your intercession, to be holy, zealous, and chaste. Make them models of virtue in the service of God's people.

Help them be pious in meditation, efficacious in preaching, and zealous in the daily offering of the Holy Sacrifice of the Mass. Help them administer the sacraments with joy.

Amen.

(St. Charles Borromeo, 1538-1584, an Italian cardinal, helped complete the work of the Council of Trent and encouraged the education of the clergy. Feast: November 4.)

Prayer for Vocations to the Priesthood

Lord Jesus Christ, Shepherd of souls, who called the apostles to be fishers of men, raise up new apostles in your holy Church. Teach them that to serve you is to reign: to possess you is to possess all things. Kindle in the hearts of our people the fire of zeal for souls. Make them eager to spread your Kingdom upon earth. Grant them courage to follow you, who are the Way, the Truth and the Life; who lives and reigns for ever and ever.

Amen.[8]

Prayer for One's Vocation in Life

Lord, make me a better person: more considerate towards others, more honest with myself, more faithful to you. Help me to find my true vocation in life and grant that through it I may find happiness myself and bring happiness to others. Grant, Lord, that those whom you call to enter priesthood or religious life may have the generosity to answer your call, so that those who need your help may always find it. We ask this through Christ our Lord.

Amen.[9]

Prayer for the Missions

O God, who would have all His children to be saved and to come to the knowledge of the truth, send forth, we beseech you, laborers into your harvest and grant them with all confidence to preach the Word; that everywhere your Gospel may be heard and glorified, and that all nations may know you, the one True God, and Him whom you have sent, Jesus Christ, your Son, our Lord.

Amen.[10]

FOR CONVERSIONS

A Prayer for Conversions

This prayer may be recited daily in September for the success of R.C.I.A. or inquiry classes:

O Blessed Apostle, St. Paul, greatest of all converts, who labored unceasingly for the conversion of other souls, inspire me with the ardor of your zeal that I may pray and work for the conversion of my brethren, redeemed in the Blood of Christ but not as yet blessed with the full light of His Truth. Mindful of the loving concern of the Divine Shepherd for the salvation of the "other sheep that are not of this fold," I now beg your intercession to obtain the grace of conversion for *(name of family member, friend or others)*. May God, the Holy Spirit from Whom alone this gift can come, hear my humble prayer and thus enable me to share with others the riches of my heritage of faith through Jesus Christ, Our Lord.

Amen.[11]

FOR HUMAN LIFE

Prayer to St. Gerard Majella for the Pro-Life Movement

St. Gerard Majella, women the world over have adopted you as their patron in the joys and fears of childbearing. Today, we invoke your intercession for the pro-life movement. Pray that all will look upon human life as a great gift from God to be accepted and loved, not as an unwanted burden to be destroyed. Assist from heaven the efforts of those on earth who are enlisted in the Christlike crusade of promoting the dignity and value of all human life, particularly the unborn. This we ask through Christ, our Lord.

Amen.

Prayer for Life

By Archbishop Fulton J. Sheen

We believe all life is precious from conception through old age to natural death. Please join in praying for the protection of the unborn. To help stop the anti-life push in the United States, Archbishop Fulton J. Sheen (who was declared "venerable" in 2012) encouraged the spiritual adoption of an unborn child. Pray that one particular but unknown child's life be spared from abortion and be allowed to continue to live. It is recommended that an individual say the following prayer for a period of one year:

Jesus, Mary, and Joseph, I love you very much. I beg you to spare the life of the unborn baby that I have spiritually adopted who is in danger of abortion.

Prayer for Respect of Life

Heavenly Father, the beauty and dignity of human life was the crowning of your creation. You further ennobled that life when your Son became one with us in his incarnation. Help us to realize the sacredness of human life and to respect it from the moment of conception until the last moment at death. Give us courage to speak with truth and love and with conviction in defense of life. Help us to extend the gentle hand of mercy and forgiveness to those who do not reverence your gift of life. To all, grant pardon for the times we have failed to be grateful for your precious gift of life or to respect it in others. We ask this in Jesus' Name. Amen.[12]

A Prayer for Our Earth

By Pope Francis

All-powerful God, you are present in the whole
    universe
and in the smallest of your creatures.
You embrace with your tenderness all that exists.
Pour out upon us the power of your love,
that we may protect life and beauty.
Fill us with peace, that we may live
as brothers and sisters, harming no one.
O God of the poor,
help us to rescue the abandoned and forgotten
    of this earth,
so precious in your eyes.

Bring healing to our lives,
that we may protect the world and not prey
     on it,
that we may sow beauty, not pollution and
     destruction.
Touch the hearts
of those who look only for gain
at the expense of the poor and the earth.
Teach us to discover the worth of each thing,
to be filled with awe and contemplation,
to recognize that we are profoundly united
with every creature
as we journey towards your infinite light.
We thank you for being with us each day.
Encourage us, we pray, in our struggle
for justice, love, and peace. Amen.[13]

Prayer for Climate Change

Your creative love, O God, brought forth our
     world,
Once a garden where humans
Could taste and see the goodness of the earth.

But our eyes have been blinded
to the beauty of Creation,
to the knowledge that it is Gift,
one given so that all humans may live and
     flourish.

Our indifference changes the world;
Even mighty glaciers weep now.
Our disregard for our sisters and brothers
Threatens the very skies above us.
Our passivity begins to choke us, and
The excess of our lifestyles blot out the sun.

Call us to renewal, to stewardship;
Call us to solidarity to the earth and all its
    creatures.
Give us new vision to see the fragile beauty that
    remains to us;
Give us new spiritual energy to become active
In loving the world through our daily life;
Give us new voices to speak out for
    environmental solidarity.

Bless us again with the gift
Of being a joyful community;
Bless us with a love of your Creation
And we will glimpse your Eden once again.[14]

A Christian Prayer in Union with Creation

By Pope Francis

Father, we praise you with all your creatures.
They came forth from your all-powerful hand;
they are yours, filled with your presence and your
tender love.
Praise be to you!

Son of God, Jesus,
through you all things were made.
You were formed in the womb of Mary our
Mother,
you became part of this earth,
and you gazed upon this world with human eyes.
Today you are alive in every creature
in your risen glory.
Praise be to you!

Holy Spirit, by your light
you guide this world towards the Father's love
and accompany creation as it groans in travail.
You also dwell in our hearts
and you inspire us to do what is good.
Praise be to you!

Triune Lord, wondrous community of infinite
love,
teach us to contemplate you
in the beauty of the universe,
for all things speak of you.
Awaken our praise and thankfulness
for every being that you have made.
Give us the grace to feel profoundly joined
to everything that is.

God of love, show us our place in this world
as channels of your love

for all the creatures of this earth,
for not one of them is forgotten in your sight.
Enlighten those who possess power and money
that they may avoid the sin of indifference,
that they may love the common good, advance
the weak,
and care for this world in which we live.
The poor and the earth are crying out.
O Lord, seize us with your power and light,
help us to protect all life,
to prepare for a better future,
for the coming of your Kingdom
of justice, peace, love and beauty.
Praise be to you!
Amen.[15]

FOR WORLD PEACE

Prayer for Peace by Pope St. John XXIII

Lord Jesus Christ, who are called the Prince of
Peace, who are yourself our peace and reconciliation, who so often said, "Peace to you," grant
us peace. Make all men and women witnesses of
truth, justice, and brotherly love. Banish from
their hearts whatever might endanger peace. Enlighten our rulers that they may guarantee and
defend the great gift of peace. May all peoples
on the earth become as brothers and sisters. May

longed-for peace blossom forth and reign always
over us all.

Prayer for Peace by Pope St. John Paul II

O God, Creator of the universe, who extends your
paternal concern over every creature and guides
the events of history in the goal of salvation, we
acknowledge your fatherly love when you break
the resistance of mankind and, in a world torn by
strife and discord, you make us ready for reconciliation. Renew for us the wonders of your mercy:
send forth your Spirit that He may work in the
intimacy of hearts, that enemies may begin to
dialogue, that adversaries may shake hands and
peoples may encounter one another in harmony.
May all commit themselves to the sincere search
for true peace which will extinguish all arguments,
for charity which overcomes hatred, for pardon
which disarms revenge.

Amen.

Prayer for Reconciliation

God of perfect peace,
violence and cruelty can have no part with you.
May those who are at peace with one another
hold fast to the good will that unites them;
may those who are enemies forget their hatred
    and be healed.[16]

Prayer for Dismantling Racism

By the Pax Christi Anti-Racism Team

Dear God, in our efforts to dismantle racism, we understand that we struggle not merely against flesh and blood but against powers and principalities — those institutions and systems that keep racism alive by perpetuating the lie that some members of the family are inferior and others superior.

Create in us a new mind and heart that will enable us to see brothers and sisters in the faces of those divided by racial categories.

Give us the grace and strength to rid ourselves of racial stereotypes that oppress some of us while providing entitlements to others.

Help us to create a Church and nation that embraces the hopes and fears of oppressed People of Color where we live, as well as those around the world.

Heal your family God, and make us one with you, in union with our brother Jesus, and empowered by your Holy Spirit.

Amen.[17]

Eternal, One and True Living God, the Merciful God

By Pope Francis

Almighty and eternal God,
good and merciful Father;
Creator of heaven and earth, of all that is visible
    and invisible;
God of Abraham, God of Isaac, God of Jacob,
King and Lord of the past, of the present and of
    the future;
sole judge of every man and woman,
who reward your faithful with eternal glory!
We, the descendants of Abraham according to
    our faith in you, the one God,
Jews, Christians and Muslims,
humbly stand before you
and with trust we pray to you
[for this world],
that men and women, followers of different
    religions, nations and cultures
may live here in peace and harmony.
We pray to you, O Father,
that it may be so in every country of the world!
Strengthen in each of us faith and hope,
mutual respect and sincere love
for all of our brothers and sisters.
Grant that we may dedicate ourselves
courageously to building a just society,
to being men and women of good will,

filled with mutual understanding and
    forgiveness,
patient artisans of dialogue and peace.
May each of our thoughts, words and actions
be in harmony with your holy will.
May everything be to your glory and honor and
    for our salvation.
Praise and eternal glory to you, our God!
Amen.[18]

FOR THE CORPORAL WORKS OF MERCY

FEED THE HUNGRY

Food for All

O God, you entrusted to us the fruits of all creation so that we might care for the earth and be
nourished with its bounty.

You sent us your Son to share our very flesh
and blood and to teach us your Law of Love.
Through His death and resurrection, we have been
formed into one human family.

Jesus showed great concern for those who had
no food — even transforming five loaves and two
fish into a banquet that served five thousand and
many more.

We come before you, O God, conscious of our

faults and failures, but full of hope, to share food with all members in this global family.

Through your wisdom, inspire leaders of government and of business, as well as all the world's citizens, to find just, and charitable solutions to end hunger by assuring that all people enjoy the right to food.

Thus we pray, O God, that when we present ourselves for Divine Judgment, we can proclaim ourselves as "One Human Family" with "Food for All." AMEN.[19]

GIVE DRINK TO THE THIRSTY

Send Your Living Waters

God who called us forth from the dust
And watered our lands with countless streams
    and great rivers,
We thank you for the garden you have set us to
    dwell in.

And in our thanks, we seek to be good stewards
    of your garden:
Protectors, nurturers, healers
In honor of you
In honor of the generations who tended this
    land before us
In honor of the generations to follow.

And so, as of old, we turn again to the sky:

Send your living waters upon the fields [around
    the world],
Sprinkle them again with your purifying rains.
Make your mountains fill with dancing streams,
Your valleys swell with splashing ponds,
As fertile as the River Jordan
As renewing as the waters of Baptism
As overflowing as the cup of salvation.

Feed all living things with your life sustaining
    water,
As you fill them with your grace.

And as we gaze upon a land that so thirsts for
    your water,
Let it remind us of all the thirsts in this world:
    The thirst for justice
    The thirst for peace
    The thirst for opportunity
    The thirst for reconciliation
The thirst for hope.

And when your blessings again rain from the
    sky,
As assuredly they will,
And we kneel again at the pools and fountains,
Teach us to cup our hands
And gently,
    gracefully,
        in solidarity

Turn first, and share with one another.
Amen.[20]

SHELTER THE HOMELESS

Prayer for Homeless People

Hear our prayer today for all women and men,
    boys and girls who are homeless this day.
For those sleeping under bridges, on park
    benches, in doorways or bus stations.
For those who can only find shelter for the night
    but must wander in the daytime.
For families broken because they could not
    afford to pay the rent.
For those who have no relatives or friends who
    can take them in.
For those who have no place to keep possessions
    that remind them who they are.
For those who are afraid and hopeless.
For those who have been betrayed by our social
    safety net.
For all these people, we pray that you will
    provide shelter, security and hope.
We pray for those of us with warm houses and
    comfortable beds
that we not be lulled into complacency and
    forgetfulness.
Jesus, help us to see your face in the eyes of
    every homeless person we meet

so that we may be empowered through word
    and deed,
and through the political means we have,
to bring justice and peace to those who are
    homeless. Amen.[21]

VISIT THE SICK

Prayer for When Visiting a Sick Person

Lord Jesus,
Lover of the sick,
Be with (name) in his (her) sickness.
Help him (her) to accept this illness
As a sharer in your cross,
And bring him (her) back to full health.

Lord Jesus,
We praise You,
For You are Lord forever and ever. Amen.[22]

VISIT THE PRISONERS

Prayer for Prisoners

Father of Mercy, the secrets of all hearts are known
to you alone. You know who is just and you forgive
the unjust. You alone are the Almighty Judge. We
are not worthy of judging anyone. Your mercy is
enough for sinners. Hear our prayers for those
in prison. Give them repentance and let them
believe in you. Give them patience and hope in

their sufferings, and bring them home again soon.
Comfort their near and dear ones. Let them trust
in Jesus Christ and live with hope. Amen.[23]

BURY THE DEAD

Catholic Funeral Prayer

God our Father,
Your power brings us to birth,
Your providence guides our lives,
and by Your command we return to dust.

Lord, those who die still live in Your presence,
their lives change but do not end.
I pray in hope for my family,
relatives and friends,
and for all the dead known to You alone.

In company with Christ,
Who died and now lives,
may they rejoice in Your kingdom,
where all our tears are wiped away.
Unite us together again in one family,
to sing Your praise forever and ever. Amen.

GIVE ALMS FOR THE POOR

Prayer for the Poor

O God, look upon the poverty of our hearts with
compassion and love. Enable us to give lovingly
and freely of our possessions and gifts. May those

who work with the poor and needy receive joy in this life and fullness of life forever. This we ask through the intercession of all the saints, especially of those whose legacy of service we carry on today. Grant that we may be faithful as they were faithful so that we too may live with you forever. Amen.[24]

SACRED SCRIPTURE

St. Jerome said, "Ignorance of the Scriptures is ignorance of Christ." Vatican II advised that "such is the force and power of the Word of God that it can serve ... the children of the Church as strength for their faith, food for the soul, and a pure and lasting font of spiritual life."[1]

Prayer Before Study

Let us pray.
Direct, O Lord,
  we beseech you,
  all our actions by your holy inspirations,
  and carry them on by your gracious
    assistance,
  that every prayer and work of ours
  may begin always from you,
  and by you be happily ended.

Through Christ our Lord.
Amen.
Hail Mary. Glory Be.[2]

Prayer for Insight

By Origen (c. 185-254)

May the Lord Jesus touch our eyes,
    as he did those of the blind.
Then shall we begin to see in visible things
    those which are invisible.
May he open our eyes to gaze,
    not on present realities,
    but on the blessings to come.
May he open the eyes of our heart
    to contemplate God in Spirit,
    through Jesus Christ the Lord,
    to whom belong power and glory
    through all eternity.[3]

Prayer for Knowledge of Scripture

Attributed to Origen

Lord, inspire us to read your Scriptures and to meditate upon them day and night. We beg you to give us real understanding of what we need, that we in turn may put its precepts into practice. Yet we know that understanding and good intentions are worthless, unless rooted in your graceful love. So we ask that the words of Scripture may also be not just signs on a page, but channels of grace into our hearts.

    Amen.[4]

——— Scripture Reading ———
as Prayer

For Discernment

Matthew 11:25

Jesus declared, "I thank you, Father, Lord of heaven and earth, that you have hidden these things from the wise and understanding and revealed them to infants." (RSV-SCE)

Colossians 1:9-14

And so, from the day we heard of it, we have not ceased to pray for you, asking that you may be filled with the knowledge of his will in all spiritual wisdom and understanding, to lead a life worthy of the Lord, fully pleasing to him, bearing fruit in every good work and increasing in the knowledge of God. May you be strengthened with all power, according to his glorious might, for all endurance and patience with joy, giving thanks to the Father, who has qualified us to share in the inheritance of the saints in light. He has delivered us from the dominion of darkness and transferred us to the kingdom of his beloved Son, in whom we have redemption, the forgiveness of sins.

James 1:2-5

Count it all joy, my brethren, when you meet various trials, for you know that the testing of your faith produces steadfastness. And let steadfastness have its full effect, that you may be perfect and complete, lacking in nothing. If any of you lacks wisdom, let him ask God, who gives to all men generously and without reproaching, and it will be given him.

For Good Works

2 Corinthians 9:6-9

The point is this: he who sows sparingly will also reap sparingly, and he who sows bountifully will also reap bountifully. Each one must do as he has made up his mind, not reluctantly or under compulsion, for God loves a cheerful giver. And God is able to provide you with every blessing in abundance, so that you may always have enough of everything and may provide in abundance for every good work. As it is written, "He scatters abroad, he gives to the poor; his righteousness endures for ever."

1 Thessalonians 1:2-4

We give thanks to God always for you all, constantly mentioning you in our prayers, remembering before our God and Father your work of faith and labor of love and steadfastness of hope in our Lord Jesus Christ. For we know, brethren beloved by God, that he has chosen you.

Colossians 3:23-24

Whatever your task, work heartily, as serving the Lord and not men, knowing that from the Lord you will receive the inheritance as your reward; you are serving the Lord Christ.

Matthew 25:40

"And the King will answer them, 'Truly, I say to you, as you did it to one of the least of these my brethren, you did it to me.'"

FOR GROWING IN FAITH

Isaiah 54:13

"All your sons shall be taught by the LORD,
    and great shall be the prosperity of your
        sons."

John 15:10-11

"If you keep my commandments, you will abide in my love, just as I have kept my Father's commandments and abide in his love. These things I have spoken to you, that my joy may be in you, and that your joy may be full."

2 Peter 3:18

[G]row in the grace and knowledge of our Lord and Savior Jesus Christ. To him be the glory both now and to the day of eternity. Amen.

Hebrews 11:1

Now faith is the assurance of things hoped for, the conviction of things not seen.

FOR STEWARDSHIP

Matthew 6:31-33

"Therefore do not be anxious, saying, 'What shall we eat?' or 'What shall we drink?' or 'What shall we wear?' For the Gentiles seek all these things; and your heavenly Father knows that you need them all. But seek first his kingdom and his righteousness, and all these things shall be yours as well."

Luke 12:33-34

"Sell your possessions, and give alms; provide yourselves with purses that do not grow old, with a treasure in the heavens that does not fail, where no thief approaches and no moth destroys. For where your treasure is, there will your heart be also."

1 Peter 4:9-11

Practice hospitality ungrudgingly to one another. As each has received a gift, employ it for one another, as good stewards of God's varied grace: whoever speaks, as one who utters oracles of God; whoever renders service, as one who renders it by the strength which God supplies; in order that in everything God may be glorified through Jesus Christ. To him belong glory and dominion for ever and ever. Amen.

Philippians 4:19-20

And my God will supply every need of yours according to his riches in glory in Christ Jesus. To our God and Father be glory for ever and ever. Amen.

FOR FAMILY
Genesis 2:18, 24

Then the LORD God said, "It is not good that the man should be alone; I will make him a helper fit for him." ... Therefore a man leaves his father and his mother and cleaves to his wife, and they become one flesh.

Exodus 20:12

"Honor your father and your mother, that your days may be long in the land which the LORD your God gives you."

Psalm 115:14

May the LORD give you increase,
  you and your children.
May you be blessed by the LORD,
  who made heaven and earth!

Psalm 128:1-6

Blessed is every one who fears the LORD,
  who walks in his ways!
You shall eat the fruit of the labor of your
    hands;
    you shall be happy, and it shall be well with
      you.

Your wife will be like a fruitful vine within your
    house;
your children will be like olive shoots around
    your table.
Lo, thus shall the man be blessed who fears the
    LORD.

The LORD bless you from Zion!
  May you see the prosperity of Jerusalem
  all the days of your life!
May you see your children's children!
  Peace be upon Israel!

PRAYERS FROM THE PSALMS

St. Ambrose asks the question: "What is more pleasing than a psalm?" and then answers, "Yes, a psalm is a blessing on the lips of the people, praise of God, the assembly's homage, a general acclamation, a word that speaks for all, the voice of the Church, a confession of faith in song."[5]

Psalm 23
Psalm of Comfort

The LORD is my shepherd, I shall not want.
  He makes me lie down in green pastures;
he leads me beside still waters;
  he restores my soul.
He leads me in paths of righteousness
  for his name's sake.

Even though I walk through the valley of the
    shadow of death,
  I fear no evil;
for you are with me;
  your rod and your staff,
    they comfort me.

You prepare a table before me
  in the presence of my enemies;
you anoint my head with oil;
  my cup overflows.

Surely goodness and mercy shall follow me
    all the days of my life,
and I shall dwell in the house of the LORD
    for ever. (RSV-SCE)

Psalm 25:1-7
Psalm of Hope

To you, O LORD, I lift up my soul.
O my God, in you I trust;
let me not be put to shame;
let not my enemies exult over me.
Yes, let none that wait for you be put to shame;
let them be ashamed who are wantonly
    treacherous.

Make me to know your ways, O LORD;
    teach me your paths.
Lead me in your truth, and teach me,
    for you are the God of my salvation;
    for you I wait all the day long.

Be mindful of your compassion, O LORD, and
    of your merciful love,
    for they have been from of old.
Remember not the sins of my youth, or my
    transgressions;
    according to your mercy remember me,
    for your goodness' sake, O LORD!
        (RSV-SCE)

Psalm 30:4-5
Psalm of Praise

Sing praises to the Lord, O you his saints,
    and give thanks to his holy name.
For his anger is but for a moment,
    and his favor is for a lifetime.
Weeping may tarry for the night,
    but joy comes with the morning.

Psalm 31:1-5
Psalm of Comfort

In you, O Lord, I seek refuge;
    let me never be put to shame;
    in your righteousness deliver me!
Incline your ear to me,
    rescue me speedily!
Be a rock of refuge for me,
    a strong fortress to save me!

Yes, you are my rock and my fortress;
    for your name's sake lead me and guide me,
take me out of the net which is hidden for me,
    for you are my refuge.
Into your hand I commit my spirit;
    you have redeemed me, O Lord, faithful
        God. (RSV-SCE)

Psalm 34:1-4
Psalm of Thanksgiving

I will bless the Lord at all times;
    his praise shall continually be in my mouth.
My soul makes its boast in the Lord;
    let the afflicted hear and be glad.
O magnify the Lord with me,
    and let us exalt his name together.

I sought the Lord, and he answered me,
    and delivered me from all my fears.

Psalm 51:1-12
Psalm of Repentance

Have mercy on me, O God,
    according to your merciful love;
according to your abundant mercy blot out my
    transgressions.
Wash me thoroughly from my iniquity,
    and cleanse me from my sin!

For I know my transgressions,
    and my sin is ever before me.
Against you, you only, have I sinned,
    and done that which is evil in your sight,
so that you are justified in your sentence
    and blameless in your judgment.
Behold, I was brought forth in iniquity,
    and in sin did my mother conceive me.

Behold, you desire truth in the inward being;
therefore teach me wisdom in my secret
heart.
Purge me with hyssop, and I shall be clean;
wash me, and I shall be whiter than snow.
Make me hear joy and gladness;
let the bones which you have broken rejoice.
Hide your face from my sins,
and blot out all my iniquities.

Create in me a clean heart, O God,
and put a new and right spirit within me.
Cast me not away from your presence,
and take not your holy Spirit from me.
Restore to me the joy of your salvation,
and uphold me with a willing spirit. (RSV-
SCE)

Psalm 71:1-21
Psalm of Hope and Patience in Tribulation

In you, O Lord, I take refuge;
let me never be put to shame!
In your righteousness deliver me and rescue me;
incline your ear to me, and save me!
Be to me a rock of refuge,
a strong fortress, to save me,
for you are my rock and my fortress.

Rescue me, O my God, from the hand of the
    wicked,
    from the grasp of the unjust and cruel man.
For you, O LORD, are my hope,
    my trust, O LORD, from my youth.
Upon you I have leaned from my birth;
    from my mother's womb, you have been my
        strength.
My praise is continually of you.

I have been as a portent to many;
    but you are my strong refuge.
My mouth is filled with your praise,
    and with your glory all the day.
Do not cast me off in the time of old age;
    forsake me not when my strength is spent.
For my enemies speak concerning me,
    those who watch for my life consult together,
and say, "God has forsaken him;
    pursue and seize him,
    for there is none to deliver him."

O God, be not far from me;
    O my God, make haste to help me!
May my accusers be put to shame and
    consumed;
    with scorn and disgrace may they be covered
    who seek my harm.
But I will hope continually,
    and will praise you yet more and more.

My mouth will tell of your righteous acts,
　of your deeds of salvation all the day,
　for their number is past my knowledge.
With the mighty deeds of the Lord GOD I will
　come,
　I will praise your righteousness, yours alone.
O God, from my youth you have taught me,
　and I still proclaim your wondrous deeds.
So even to old age and gray hairs,
　O God, do not forsake me,
till I proclaim your might
　to all the generations to come.
Your power and your righteousness, O God,
　reach the high heavens.

You who have done great things,
　O God, who is like you?
You who have made me see many sore troubles
　will revive me again;
from the depths of the earth
　you will bring me up again.
You will increase my honor,
　and comfort me again. (RSV-SCE)

Psalm 86:1-12
Psalm of Petition

Incline your ear, O LORD, and answer me,
　for I am poor and needy.
Preserve my life, for I am godly;
　save your servant who trusts in you.

You are my God; have mercy on me, O Lord,
    for to you do I cry all the day.
Gladden the soul of your servant,
    for to you, O Lord, do I lift up my soul.
For you, O Lord, are good and forgiving,
    abounding in mercy to all who call on you.
Give ear, O Lord, to my prayer;
    listen to my cry of supplication.
In the day of my trouble I call on you,
    for you do answer me.

There is none like you among the gods, O Lord,
    nor are there any works like yours.
All the nations you have made shall come
    and bow down before you, O Lord,
    and shall glorify your name.
For you are great and do wondrous things,
    you alone are God.
Teach me your way, O Lord,
    that I may walk in your truth;
    unite my heart to fear your name.
I give thanks to you, O Lord my God, with my
    whole heart,
    and I will glorify your name for ever. (RSV-
    SCE)

Psalm 91
A Lenten and Night Psalm

He who dwells in the shelter of the Most High,
who abides in the shadow of the Almighty,
will say to the LORD, "My refuge and my
fortress;
my God, in whom I trust."
For he will deliver you from the snare of the
fowler
and from the deadly pestilence;
he will cover you with his pinions,
and under his wings you will find refuge;
his faithfulness is a shield and buckler.
You will not fear the terror of the night,
nor the arrow that flies by day,
nor the pestilence that stalks in darkness,
nor the destruction that wastes at noonday.

A thousand may fall at your side,
ten thousand at your right hand;
but it will not come near you.
You will only look with your eyes
and see the recompense of the wicked.

Because you have made the LORD your refuge,
the Most High your habitation,
no evil shall befall you,
no scourge come near your tent.

For he will give his angels charge of you
>   to guard you in all your ways.
On their hands they will bear you up,
>   lest you dash your foot against a stone.
You will tread on the lion and the adder,
>   the young lion and the serpent you will
>   trample under foot.

Because he cleaves to me in love, I will deliver
>   him;
>   I will protect him, because he knows my
>   name.
When he calls to me, I will answer him;
>   I will be with him in trouble,
>   I will rescue him and honor him.
With long life I will satisfy him,
>   and show him my salvation.

Psalm 100
A Song of Praise; A Morning Prayer

Make a joyful noise to the LORD, all the lands!
>   Serve the LORD with gladness!
>   Come into his presence with singing!

Know that the LORD is God!
>   It is he that made us, and we are his;
>   we are his people, and the sheep of his
>   pasture.

Enter his gates with thanksgiving,
    and his courts with praise!
    Give thanks to him, bless his name!

For the LORD is good;
    his steadfast love endures for ever,
    and his faithfulness to all generations.

Psalm 123
Psalm of Mercy

To you I lift up my eyes,
    O you who are enthroned in the heavens!
Behold, as the eyes of servants
    look to the hand of their master,
as the eyes of a maid
    to the hand of her mistress,
so our eyes look to the LORD our God,
    till he have mercy upon us.

Have mercy upon us, O LORD, have mercy
    upon us,
    for we have had more than enough of
        contempt.
Too long our soul has been sated
    with the scorn of those who are at ease,
    the contempt of the proud. (RSV-SCE)

Psalm 130 (*De Profundis*)
In Difficult Times

Out of the depths I cry to you, O Lord!
    Lord, hear my voice!
Let your ears be attentive
    to the voice of my supplications!

If you, O Lord, should mark iniquities,
    Lord, who could stand?
But there is forgiveness with you,
    so that you may be feared.

I wait for the Lord, my soul waits,
    and in his word I hope;
my soul waits for the Lord
    more than watchmen for the morning,
    more than watchmen for the morning.

O Israel, hope in the Lord!
    For with the Lord there is mercy,
    and with him is plenteous redemption.
And he will redeem Israel
from all his iniquities. (RSV-SCE)

Psalm 136:1-3
God's Love for Us

O give thanks to the Lord, for he is good,
    for his steadfast love endures for ever.
O give thanks to the God of gods,
    for his steadfast love endures for ever.

O give thanks to the Lord of lords,
    for his steadfast love endures for ever.

Psalm 137:1-7
Spiritual Comfort

By the waters of Babylon, there we sat down and
    wept,
    when we remembered Zion.
On the willows there
    we hung up our lyres.
For there our captors
    required of us songs,
and our tormentors, mirth, saying,
    "Sing us one of the songs of Zion!"

How shall we sing the LORD's song
    in a foreign land?
If I forget you, O Jerusalem,
    let my right hand wither!
Let my tongue cleave to the roof of my mouth,
    if I do not remember you,
if I do not set Jerusalem
    above my highest joy!

Remember, O LORD, against the Edomites
    the day of Jerusalem,
how they said, "Raze it, raze it!
    Down to its foundations!"

Psalm 141
Evening Prayer of Repentance

I call upon you, O LORD; make haste to help me!
  Give ear to my voice when I call to you!
Let my prayer be counted as incense before you,
  and the lifting up of my hands as an evening
    sacrifice!

Set a guard over my mouth, O LORD,
  keep watch over the door of my lips!
Incline not my heart to any evil,
  to busy myself with wicked deeds
in company with men who work iniquity;
  and let me not eat of their dainties!

Let a good man strike or rebuke me in kindness,
  but let the oil of the wicked never anoint my
    head;
    for my prayer is continually against their
      wicked deeds.
When they are given over to those who shall
    condemn them,
  then they shall learn that the word of the
    LORD is true.
As a rock which one cleaves and shatters on the land,
  so shall their bones be strewn at the mouth
    of Sheol.

But my eyes are toward you, O LORD God;
  in you I seek refuge; leave me not defenseless!

Keep me from the trap which they have laid
    for me,
    and from the snares of evildoers!
Let the wicked together fall into their own nets,
    while I escape. (RSV-SCE)

Psalm 143:8-10
For Guidance

Let me hear in the morning of your merciful love,
    for in you I put my trust.
Teach me the way I should go,
    for to you I lift up my soul.

Deliver me, O LORD, from my enemies!
    I have fled to you for refuge!
Teach me to do your will,
    for you are my God!
Let your good spirit lead me
    on a level path! (RSV-SCE)

Psalm 148
Psalm of Praise and Glory

Praise the LORD!
    Praise the LORD from the heavens,
    praise him in the heights!
Praise him, all his angels,
    praise him, all his host!

Praise him, sun and moon,
    praise him, all you shining stars!

Praise him, you highest heavens,
and you waters above the heavens!

Let them praise the name of the LORD!
For he commanded and they were created.
And he established them for ever and ever;
he fixed their bounds, which cannot be passed.

Praise the LORD from the earth,
you sea monsters and all deeps,
fire and hail, snow and frost,
stormy wind fulfilling his command!

Mountains and all hills,
fruit trees and all cedars!
Beasts and all cattle,
creeping things and flying birds!

Kings of the earth and all peoples,
princes and all rulers of the earth!
Young men and maidens together,
old men and children!

Let them praise the name of the LORD,
for his name alone is exalted;
his glory is above earth and heaven.
He has raised up a horn for his people,
praise for all his saints,
for the people of Israel who are near to him.
Praise the LORD!

Psalm 150
A Hymn of Praise

Praise the LORD!
Praise God in his sanctuary;
    praise him in his mighty firmament!
Praise him for his mighty deeds;
    praise him according to his exceeding
      greatness!

Praise him with trumpet sound;
    praise him with lute and harp!
Praise him with timbrel and dance;
    praise him with strings and pipe!
Praise him with sounding cymbals;
    praise him with loud clashing cymbals!
Let everything that breathes praise the LORD!
Praise the LORD!

ACKNOWLEDGMENTS

The editor is most grateful to those listed in "Notes (Sources for Texts)" and to the following sources for the use of prayers, other texts, and information:

- Unless otherwise noted, quotations from papal and other Vatican-generated documents are available on vatican.va and copyright © Libreria Editrice Vaticana.
- English translation of the *Catechism of the Catholic Church* for use in the United States of America copyright © 1994, United States Catholic Conference, Inc. — Libreria Editrice Vaticana. English translation of the *Catechism of the Catholic Church: Modifications from the Editio Typica* copyright © 1997, United States Catholic Conference, Inc. — Libreria Editrice Vaticana.
- The English translations of the *Te Deum*, Lamb of God, the *Benedictus*, the *Magnificat*, and the *Nunc Dimittis* are by the English Language Liturgical Consultation (ELLC).

- Unless otherwise noted, the Scripture citations used in this work are taken from the *Catholic Edition of the Revised Standard Version of the Bible* (RSV), copyright © 1965 and 1966 by the National Council of the Churches of Christ in the United States of America. Used by permission. All rights reserved. Where noted, other Scripture citations are from the *Revised Standard Version of the Bible — Second Catholic Edition* (Ignatius Edition), designated as RSV-SCE, copyright © 2006 National Council of the Churches of Christ in the United States of America. Used by permission. All rights reserved.

NOTES
(SOURCES FOR TEXTS)

Basic Prayers

1. From *The Roman Missal*, copyright © 2010, International Commission on English in the Liturgy Corporation (ICEL). All rights reserved.

Blessed Trinity

1. English translation of the *Te Deum* by the English Language Liturgical Consultation (ELLC).
2. From *Handbook of Prayers*, Rev. James Socías, general editor (Huntington, IN: Our Sunday Visitor, Inc.; Princeton, NJ: Scepter Publishers, Inc.; Chicago: Midwest Theological Forum, 2001).
3. From *Manual of Prayers*, compiled by Rev. James D. Watkins (Rome: Pontifical North American College, 1998; published in the United States by Midwest Theological Forum, Chicago).
4. Ibid.
5. Ibid.
6. From the 1841 Armenian liturgy translation of John Mason Neale in E .F. K. Fortescue, *The Armenian Church* (London: J.T. Hayes, 1872; rpt. New York: AMS Press, Inc., 1970), pp. 105-106 (English modernized).

Blessed Virgin Mary

1. From *A Prayer Book for Young Catholics*, by Father Robert Fox (Huntington, IN: Our Sunday Visitor, 1981).
2. From *Evangelium Vitae* ("The Gospel of Life"), n. 105.

Saints and Holy Ones

1. From *Manual of Prayers*.
2. Ibid.
3. Ibid.
4. Ibid.
5. From Prayers4reparation's blog.
6. From *Manual of Prayers*.
7. Ibid.
8. From the United States Conference of Catholic Bishops (USCCB).
9. From *Manual of Prayers*.
10. Ibid.
11. From *Mother Teresa's Secret Fire: The Encounter That Changed St. Teresa of Calcutta's Life and How It Can Transform Your Own,* by Joseph Langford (Huntington, IN: Our Sunday Visitor, 2008, 2016).
12. From *Manual of Prayers*.
13. Ibid.
14. Ibid.
15. From *Prayer Book of the Saints*, by Rev. Charles Dollen (Huntington, IN: Our Sunday Visitor, 1984).

Litanies

1. Adapted from *A Book of Prayers*, copyright © 1982, ICEL. All rights reserved.
2. Adapted from *Pastoral Care of the Sick: Rites of Anointing and Viaticum*, copyright © 1982, ICEL. All rights reserved.

Novena Prayers

1. From *Novenas for the Church Year*, by Fr. Peter John Cameron (Huntington, IN: Our Sunday Visitor, 2012).
2. From *Manual of Prayers*.
3. Translation by Mario H. Ibertis Rivera, founder of the International Fraternity of the Virgin Mary, Untier of Knots.
4. From www.usccb.org.
5. From the Father Solanus Guild.

Mass

1. From *Holy Communion and Worship of the Eucharist Outside Mass*, copyright © 1974, ICEL. All rights reserved.
2. From *Padre Pio's Words of Hope*, by Eileen Dunn Bertanzetti (Huntington, IN: Our Sunday Visitor, 1999).
3. From *The Roman Missal*.
4. Ibid.
5. Ibid.
6. Ibid.
7. English translation of Lamb of God by the ELLC.
8. From *The Roman Missal*.
9. Based on a prayer from an earlier edition of *The Roman Missal*.

Prayers Throughout the Day

1. From *Manual of Prayers*.
2. English translation of the *Benedictus* by the ELLC.
3. From *Manual of Prayers*.
4. Probably written by Heartsill Wilson.
5. Adapted from *Book of Blessings*, copyright © 1987, ICEL. All rights reserved.
6. From *A Book of Prayers*.

7. English translation of the *Magnificat* by the ELLC.
8. English translation of the *Nunc Dimittis* by the ELLC.

Prayers Throughout the Year

1. From *The Liturgy of the Hours*, © 1973, 1974, 1975, ICEL. All rights reserved.
2. From *The Catholic Parent Book of Feasts: Celebrating the Church Year with Your Family*, by Michaelann Martin, Carol Puccio, and Zoë Romanowsky (Huntington, IN: Our Sunday Visitor, 1999).
3. From *Manual of Prayers*.
4. From St. John Paul II's *Insegnamenti* (Dec. 31, 1979) in *John Paul II's Book of Mary*, compiled by Margaret R. Bunson (Huntington, IN: Our Sunday Visitor, 1996).
5. Prayer by David Philippart in *Welcome Yule! 1995* (Chicago: Liturgy Training Publications, 1994).
6. Adapted from *Catholic Household Blessings & Prayers, Revised Edition* (Washington, DC: United States Conference of Catholic Bishops [USCCB], 2007).
7. From *A Prayer Book for Young Catholics*.
8. From *Catholic Household Blessings & Prayers*.
9. From *The Liturgy of the Hours*. (See Philippians 2:8-9.)
10. Translated from the Italian by Edward Caswall (1814-1878).
11. From *Rite of Holy Week*, copyright © 1970, ICEL.
12. *A Catholic Book of Hours and Other Devotions*, by William G. Storey (Chicago, IL: Loyola Press, 2007).
13. Adapted from *Catholic Household Blessings & Prayers, Revised Edition*.
14. From *Book of Common Prayer*.
15. From *The Liturgy of the Hours*.
16. Ibid.
17. From *A Book of Prayers*.

18. From *The Roman Missal*.
19. From *Catholic Household Blessings & Prayers, Revised Edition*.
20. Ibid.
21. From St. Joseph's Oratory of Mount Royal, Montreal QC H3V1 H6.
22. From *Manual of Prayers*.
23. From *The Liturgy of the Hours*.
24. From the USCCB website http://www.usccb.org/issues-and-action/religious-liberty/our-first-most-cherished-liberty.cfm. Used by permission.
25. From *The Roman Missal*.
26. From *Embraced by Mary: Marian Devotions and Prayers Throughout the Year*, by Rawley Myers (Huntington, IN: Our Sunday Visitor, 1997).
27. March 1958. From Libreria Editrice Vaticana.
28. From Sisters of Providence of Saint Mary-of-the-Woods in Indiana.
29. From *Order of Christian Funerals*, copyright © 1985, ICEL.
30. From *Catholic Household Blessings & Prayers, Revised Edition*.
31. From *The Roman Missal*.

Special Occasions

1. From *Manuscrits autobiographiques*, C 25r.
2. Adapted from *Book of Blessings*.
3. From *A Prayer Book for Young Catholics*.
4. Adapted from the French by Dr. Chau Thien Phan, Rider University, Lawrenceville, NJ 08648: "*Prières apostoliques: Lumière, Sel, Levain*," Fernand Lelotte, S.J., in *Rabboni: Consignes et prières pour mieux servir* (Paris: Casterman, 1958).

5. From *Manual of Prayers*.
6. Adapted from *Book of Blessings*.
7. From *Manual of Prayers*.
8. From the USCCB website http://www.usccb.org/prayer-and -worship/prayers-and-devotions/prayers/prayer-for-troops .cfm.
9. From *Manual of Prayers*.
10. From *Day by Day: The Notre Dame Prayerbook for Students*, edited by Thomas McNally and William G. Storey (Notre Dame, IN: Ave Maria Press, 1975).
11. From *Prayers in Times of Crisis* (Chicago: Liturgy Training Publications, 2003).
12. From Mariannhill Missionaries.
13. From *Manual of Prayers*.
14. From *The Catholic Parent Book of Feasts*.
15. From *The Pope's Family Prayer Book* (Libreria Editrice Vaticana, 1976).
16. Ibid.
17. From *Pastoral Care of the Sick: Rites of Anointing and Viaticum*.
18. From Friends of St. John the Caregiver, www.FSJC.org.
19. From the Catholic Healing Ministry of Baltimore, MD.
20. From ICEL.
21. From *Prayers Out of the Depths* (Chicago: Liturgical Training Publications, 2003).
22. From *Pastoral Care of the Sick: Rites of Anointing and Viaticum*.
23. From *Manual of Prayers*.
24. Adapted from *Book of Blessings*.
25. From Friends of St. John the Caregiver, www.FSJC.org.
26. From *Handbook of Prayers*.

27. From *Pastoral Care of the Sick: Rites of Anointing and Viaticum*.
28. From *Order of Christian Funerals*.
29. From *The Roman Missal*.
30. From *Pastoral Care of the Sick: Rites of Anointing and Viaticum*.
31. From *Order of Christian Funerals*.
32. Ibid.

Consecrations

1. From *Manual of Prayers*.

Prayers for the Church and the World

1. From *Manual of Prayers*.
2. Ibid.
3. From *The Roman Missal*.
4. Ibid.
5. From *Manual of Prayers*.
6. Ibid.
7. From *Lumen Gentium* (Dogmatic Constitution on the Church), n. 18.
8. From *Handbook of Prayers*.
9. From *Manual of Prayers*.
10. Ibid.
11. From the Diocese of Fort Wayne, August 15, 1958.
12. From Catholic Online, www.catholic.org. Reprinted with permission.
13. From *Laudato Si'* (on care for our common home), n. 246.
14. By Jane Deren, 2009, copyright © www.educationfor justice.org.
15. From *Laudato Si'*, n. 246.
16. From *The Liturgy of the Hours*.

17. From Pax Christi USA.

18. From an address, June 6, 2015.

19. From Caritas, www.caritas.org. Emphasis is in the original text.

20. From Catholic Relief Services.

21. From Leading in Worship, a Mennonite prayer resource.

22. From Catholic Online, www.catholic.org. Reprinted with permission.

23. From www.LordCalls.com.

24. From e-Catholic2000.com.

Sacred Scripture

1. From *Dei Verbum* (Dogmatic Constitution on Divine Revelation), n. 21.

2. From *Manual of Prayers*.

3. Ibid.

4. Ibid.

5. From *In psalmum I enarratio*, 1, 9.

INDEX

Charity, Act of — 15

Charles Borromeo, St. — 303

Charles de Foucauld, Bl. — 169

Child, Daily Blessing of a — 271

Children — 269-273

Christ Crucified, Prayer to — 156-157

Christian Unity, Prayer for — 216, 298

Christmas — 188-191

    Novena — 189

    Prayer by Gerard Manley Hopkins — 189

    Twelve Days of — 190

Christopher, St. — 60

Clare of Assisi, St. — 60-61, 202-203

Clement of Alexandria, St. — 61-62

Clement of Rome, St. — 61

Clement XI, Universal Prayer by Pope — 158-161

Clergy, Prayer for the Sanctification of the — 302

Climate Change — 308-309

Colossians 1:9-14 — 325

Colossians 3:23-24 — 327

Columba Marmion, O.S.B., Bl. — 193-194

Come, Holy Spirit — 30

Come, Holy Spirit, Creator Blest — 33-34

Comfort, Psalm of — 331-333

Comfort, Spiritual — 343

Coming Home Each Day, Prayer at — 177

Commendation, Prayers of — 285

Communion Fast, Prayer During — 145

Communion, Personal Prayer after — 155 (for a Spiritual
    Communion prayer, see St. Francis of Assisi, 66)

Communion, Prayer for the Promotion of Daily — 149-150

Confiteor — 151

Consecrations — 293-296

    for the United States — 265

    in the Sacred Heart of Jesus — 294-295

    of the Family — 295-296